Praise for *Live to Give*

"Austin and his family are an inspiration to all of us. Can one person make a huge difference? Austin proves the answer is YES."

—MAX LUCADO, MINISTER OF PREACHING AT OAK HILLS CHURCH IN SAN ANTONIO, TEXAS

"Austin Gutwein has been changing the world in a big way since he was thirteen. *Live to Give* is not an ordinary book. This is Austin's already successful blueprint for a generation of young people. And their parents!"

—ANDY ANDREWS, *NEW YORK TIMES* BEST-SELLING AUTHOR OF *HOW DO YOU KILL 11 MILLION PEOPLE?*, *THE NOTICER*, AND *THE TRAVELER'S GIFT*

"Austin Gutwein is a hero with a powerful message for his generation—and anyone else with the courage to give their lives for others!"

—RICHARD STEARNS, PRESIDENT OF WORLD VISION US AND AUTHOR OF *THE HOLE IN OUR GOSPEL*

". . . If all who read this book actually apply the principles and practices suggested, I believe we will see world-impacting blessing and a great advancement of God's Kingdom."

—DAVID WRAIGHT, YOUTH FOR CHRIST INTERNATIONAL PRESIDENT

"This book is delightfully practical! In a world that is searching for identity, Austin offers simple, yet profound insights about discovering who you are (what's in your lunch box) and how to live it out. I've been deeply impacted by the truths articulated in *Live to Give*. Get it . . . read it . . . live it."

—JEFF GOKEE, EXECUTIVE DIRECTOR OF PHOENIXONE

LIVE
TO
GIVE

LET GOD
TURN YOUR
TALENTS
INTO
MIRACLES

AUSTIN GUTWEIN

THOMAS NELSON
Since 1798

NASHVILLE   DALLAS   MEXICO CITY   RIO DE JANEIRO

Published in Nashville, Tennessee, by Tommy Nelson. Tommy Nelson is a registered trademark of Thomas Nelson, Inc.

Author is represented by the literary agency of Alive Communications, Inc., 7680 Goddard Street, Suite 200, Colorado Springs, CO 80920, www.alivecommunications.com.

Tommy Nelson® titles may be purchased in bulk for educational, business, fund-raising, or sales promotional use. For information, please e-mail SpecialMarkets@ThomasNelson.com.

Library of Congress Cataloging-in-Publication Data

Gutwein, Austin.
  Live to give : let God turn your talents into miracles / Austin Gutwein.
    p. cm.
  Includes bibliographical references.
  ISBN 978-1-4003-1993-0 (pbk.)
  1. Service (Theology) 2. Christian teenagers—Religious life. 3. Church work. I. Title.
BT738.4.G88 2012
248.4—dc23

                                                                    2012007530

This book is dedicated to my amazing parents. Mom and Dad, thank you for always being there for me. I love you both so much, and I am so thankful for having you in my life! I am truly blessed by God.

Contents

1. Live to Give 1

2. Unique Lunch 14

3. Different Outside and In 22

4. What's in Your Lunch Box? 44

5. Don't Lose Your Lunch! 57

6. Grab Your Lunch and Hit the Road 75

7. When It Gets Bumpy 94

8. Your Biggest Fear: Fear 105

9. Hungry 120

10. The Trader 129

11. Sandwich Squasher 139

12. Give It 159

13. The Results 169

14. Our World 182

Notes 193

Acknowledgments 195

About the Author and Hoops of Hope 196

1

Live to Give

God doesn't need you.

God doesn't need you or your help to make a difference. God doesn't need you to bring an issue before the world or try to make an impact. Why? Because God is God. But even though God doesn't need you, He wants you.

I was recently in Mexico on a service project, building a house for a very poor Tijuana family. When it came time for us to finish up the project, we pulled out our paint and brushes and began to put the final touch on the house: a nice coat of watery green. All of a sudden, a few of the children who were going to live in the house showed up with huge smiles on their faces and big hearts willing to work. They wanted to paint too! So we let them help out. Sure, it may have taken a little bit longer and been a little bit messier, with paint sloshed on us and on them, but that paint job was filled with more smiles and laughter than any I've done before or since. You see, we didn't technically need their help, but we did want it.

I'm sure we've all been in those kids' shoes from time to time: trying to "help" our parents make cookies when we were really little (and getting flour everywhere), or perhaps "helping" your dad or granddad fix up an old car (and slowing down the process). See, there are much more qualified people around for jobs like that. But because these adults loved us and wanted us to learn, they let us help. I believe God feels the same way.

> He *wants* to use us, which means we *get* to work by His side and have front-row seats to see His amazing power.

The truth of the matter is that God doesn't need us because He is God—the most qualified being in the universe! But the good news is that just because God *can* do anything without us doesn't mean He *wants* to. God can create anything, fix any problem, and He can do it all without us. But He *wants* to use us, which means we *get* to work by His side and have front-row seats to see His amazing power.

Here's an example. Let's take the problem of hunger. Feeding the hungry is an overwhelming job. Did you know there are 925 million people who go hungry each and every day?[1] To put that in perspective, the United States has 308 million people. So that means that the number of people who go hungry every day is equal to the population of our entire country times three. And God could feed all of those people in a second. God's done it before. Just check out the story of Moses and the Israelites in the Bible (Exodus 16). While they were wandering around the desert for forty years, God made food drop from the sky that nobody had even seen before. The Israelites started calling it *manna*, which means "what is it?" God could drop some manna down again. Maybe even with a little hot sauce on it. But why doesn't He? I can't say for sure. We do know, though, that God *wants to use human beings* to solve the world's problems.

When God was making Adam, He said, "Let us make mankind in our image, in our likeness, so that they may rule over the fish in the sea and the birds in the sky, over the livestock and all the wild animals, and over all the creatures that move along the ground" (Genesis 1:26).

He gave Adam a mission. Then He let him name all

the animals (although I think the guy must have been hurting for names by the time he got to the dodo and the pig-footed bandicoot, don't you?). And we inherited Adam's mission to take care of things ever since. I'm pretty honored by that. God made people with giving in mind—He chose us to make a difference.

Jesus said, "You didn't choose me, remember; I chose you, and put you in the world to bear fruit, fruit that won't spoil" (John 15:16 MSG).

This means *you*! And me! God has made a plan to use *you* to accomplish eternal, life-giving, miraculous things! Now, that's pretty exciting—the most exciting thing that will ever happen to us in our whole lives!

Sure, God was perfectly capable of naming all the animals by Himself. He didn't need Adam or a team of landscapers to make the plants grow in the garden of Eden either. In the same way, God could solve the world's biggest problems in an instant, wiping out suffering and diseases as terrible as cancer or AIDS. I don't know why He doesn't. That's one of those big mysteries we'll have to ask Him about when we get to heaven. One thing I can tell you for sure is that we don't know all the answers for why God sometimes chooses not to intervene directly. But the thing we can know is that when we live to give, we get to partner with a God whose love has no end, and we get to play a part in His incredible plan—a plan that will last for eternity.

WE HAVE A PART TO PLAY

There are so many examples in the Bible of God using regular people—even kids—to help Him make amazing things happen. He could have done these things by Himself, of course, but He picked people He loved to help bring life to the world. Later, we'll talk about how you are just such a person. But first let's look at John 6 for an example of how a partnership with God works. It's the story of the feeding of the five thousand. This is one of the most amazing miracles in Jesus' lifetime. In fact, it is the only miracle, other than the resurrection, that is written about in all four gospels.[2] That means it is pretty important. And in this miracle, Jesus uses the direct help of someone else—a kid a lot like you and me. Let me paint the picture for you.

Jesus and His disciples hop into a boat and sail to the other side of the Sea of Galilee. Along the shore, people see the boat and follow it all the way to the other side of the sea! When Jesus and the disciples reach the shore, they are greeted by an ever-growing crowd estimated at five thousand men. This means there were probably many more than five thousand people overall, counting the women and children (Matthew says there were "about five thousand men, besides women and children" [14:21]). Jesus begins to heal their sick and teach them. Why? Mark 6:34 gives us the answer: "When Jesus landed and saw a large crowd, he had *compassion* on them, because they were like sheep without a shepherd."[3]

That compassion leads Him to continue teaching until very late in the day, sharing wisdom and hope. But then the disciples run into a problem. All the people who have been listening to Jesus are hungry and without food, and they are too far from home to go get any kind of quick meal. I'm pretty sure takeout wasn't around back then.

Jesus' compassion on the crowd shows itself again; He tells His disciples to go get them something to eat. Imagine! What if someone asked you to rustle up a nice dinner for, oh, ten thousand people, just on the fly? The disciples are understandably stressed—they know they can't possibly afford to feed all these people. It would take the modern-day equivalent of $8,000, or half a year's wages for them.[4] But Andrew looks around and manages to find a little boy who has what seems to be the only ounce of food around. It is a meager meal made up of only five small barley loaves and two fish—barely enough to feed the boy, let alone the huge crowd. We're not talking about a big meal by any stretch of the imagination.

But it *would* be enough—in fact, *more* than enough. Jesus uses this little boy's meal to feed the whole crowd. The Bible says Jesus gives thanks for the small lunch, the disciples divide it up, and everyone has their fill of food. Then—and this shows how great this miracle was—the disciples actually pick up twelve basketfuls of leftovers!

Jesus didn't need that boy. Jesus didn't need his lunch. He could have fed everyone without even missing a beat in His teaching. Jesus could have turned rocks into bread if He wanted to—but instead, He chose to use that boy. The Bible doesn't give us many details about this kid or why Jesus chose to use him, but I can't help but wonder if He did it to show us what happens when we offer our gifts to Him.

····•◆•····

I was nine years old, sitting on a couch in my living room with my family. The TV was on and we were all glued to it, but it wasn't a typical movie or cartoon show keeping our attention. On the screen was another nine-year-old—a little girl named Maggie. She lived almost ten thousand miles away in Zambia, and her life was about as different from mine as it could get. You see, Maggie was what's known as an AIDS orphan. She had been born to parents who both died of this horrible disease, and she was suffering because of it. Instead of having a nice house like mine, she lived under an old tarp with her great-grandmother. She huddled there without protection from the rain, without enough food to eat, enough clothes to wear, or a school to go to. When she stared into the camera, her eyes looked empty, as if she were so tired that she couldn't go on much longer. This was so scary to me. Maggie didn't ask for that life or deserve it, but there she was, staring with empty eyes under that tarp. And there I was, watching TV on a nice couch in our family room in Arizona.

Then, in the next moment, Maggie's image faded from the screen, and it seemed as though I was transported back to my normal cares and concerns. But not quite. That's when God changed things for me. All of a sudden, everything around me looked different. Maggie's story was really real—really happening on the other side of the world, and all the while I was going about my life in ease and comfort. *It could have been me*, I thought. I had to do something. And that's how it all started.

God used that moment to break my heart and start a journey that led to my first book, *Take Your Best Shot*. He used my broken heart by giving it a dream to help Maggie and others like her in a way that would let me do what I liked to do most—shoot free throws on the basketball court. He used that dream to start a crazy journey that would eventually lead to the creation of an organization called Hoops of Hope, which has helped people all over the world raise more than $2.5 million to support His kids in Africa. I don't know how He did it. All I know is that He made a miracle happen—and He still is! Over the past eight years, more than forty thousand people have joined us in raising money for AIDS orphans. God continues to work and do wonders through Hoops of Hope.

Why did Jesus use the little boy with bread and fish to feed thousands of hungry people? Why did God use a nine-year-old kid in Arizona to help AIDS orphans? Because He *wanted* to. And God wants to use *you* to make a difference too!

"*Really?*" you might say. "AIDS and hunger and things like that are huge problems. These are a big deal, and I'm just me. How could a kid like me even make a dent in such big problems?" Your question would be understandable. But don't let the fact that God wants to use you intimidate or overwhelm you. Remember Philippians 4:13: "I can do all things through Christ who strengthens me" (NKJV).

It's not you doing the heavy lifting—it's Christ, and He's got endless backup. Still feel a little puny and unsure? Look how God is described in Isaiah 40:29: "He gives strength to the weary and increases the power of the weak."

Afraid you might run out of steam? Paul wrote in Philippians, "There has never been the slightest doubt in my mind that the God who started this great work in you would keep at it and bring it to a flourishing finish on the very day Christ Jesus appears" (1:6 MSG).

God loves seeing us live our lives to the fullest by

giving of ourselves in the service of others. Sure, He could do it all on His own, but because He loves us, He wants to use us! He wants us to live to give.

A GIFT THAT KEEPS ON GIVING

What exactly does it mean to live to give? I think it starts with knowing the reason God put you on this earth. God has something for you to do, just as He had a plan for Adam and for the boy with the bread and fish. We shouldn't wait to use these gifts God has given us. The apostle Peter wrote, "Each of you should use *whatever gift you have received* to serve others, as faithful stewards of God's grace" (1 Peter 4:10, emphasis added).

That's right—you have received a gift. And it's a gift that keeps on giving, but only if you use it. Only if you give it back to Him.

When we live to give, letting God use whatever we've got, we join Him in an awesome adventure. We start working hand in hand with Him to bring about amazing, transforming, mind-blowing things in our lives and the lives of others. But before we *live* this adventure, we need to find out what God wants us to *give*.

For me, it was shooting hoops to raise money. He wanted me to give my time and my favorite hobby. For the boy in the multitude of five thousand, it was his lunch. For you . . . well, this book is meant to help you discover what that is. But there is one common theme throughout all of our stories: we all need to live to give because we were made for it. Nothing beats living this way! Nothing we could eat, drink, buy, play, watch, or win in life can compare to the feeling of giving ourselves away, using "whatever gift we have received to serve others as faithful stewards of God's grace."

WHAT ARE YOU LIVING FOR?

Before we go on and discover how we were meant to live to give, I would encourage you to answer this question: What are you living for?

What gets you going in the morning? What is your top priority? What is the most important thing in your life? Don't like your answer right now? I didn't either at first. This world is a distracting place. There's so much to entertain us, so much stuff to consume or collect, so many people to compare ourselves to. It can be tough to keep our heads clear and our hearts focused on God. Sometimes it's tough even to know what's in our heads and hearts at all. But by the end of this book, you will be able to answer two questions: What *have* I been living for? And what was I *made* to be living for?

Believe me, the answer to the second question is more exciting, fulfilling, and satisfying than anything we can get out of a box or see on TV. When we're used by God, we never know just how crazy things will get. I never thought Hoops of Hope would lead to me visiting Africa or meeting some of the most amazing, strongest people on the face of the earth. But even without those experiences, it's enough for me to know that when I live to give to God and others, He uses it for His glory. Plus, as the Bible puts it, "One who is faithful in a very little is also faithful in much" (Luke 16:10 ESV). That means that the adventure never stops. God will continue to teach and help us grow so that we're able to live and give even more: another gift that keeps on giving.

So how do we get started on this journey? What is it that *you* were meant to give? Read on, and let's find out!

STUDY QUESTIONS

1. WHAT ARE YOUR TOP FIVE PRIORITIES IN LIFE RIGHT NOW, IN ORDER? ACCORDING TO THE THINGS ON THAT LIST, WHAT DO YOU SEEM TO BE LIVING FOR?

2. HAVE YOU EVER FELT AS THOUGH SOMEONE DIDN'T NEED YOUR HELP BUT WANTED IT ANYWAY? GIVE A SPECIFIC EXAMPLE. HOW DID GETTING THE OPPORTUNITY TO HELP IN THAT SITUATION MAKE YOU FEEL?

3. IF YOU WERE TO TWEET ABOUT GOD'S AWESOMENESS, WHAT WOULD YOU TWEET?

4. WHAT DOES IT MEAN TO YOU TO KNOW THAT GOD WANTS TO USE YOU?

5. GIVE AN EXAMPLE OF A TANGIBLE GIFT THAT KEEPS ON GIVING. DO YOU BELIEVE YOU HAVE A GIFT THAT KEEPS GIVING?

2

Unique Lunch

I stood looking down at the water; it must have been close to four hundred feet below me. The river was rushing like a speeding car, only a short way away from Victoria Falls. Before I could finish gazing at the beauty of the Zambezi River, the five-second countdown began. All of a sudden, with one shove, I was falling like a rock that had been thrown from the bridge, with nothing but a thin cord keeping me from plunging into the waiting arms of the icy water far below. A lot of people might call that terrifying. Some might say it's insane. But I have one word for it: *fun*! My idea of fun may be different from, say, my grandmother's. But that's okay. It's our differences that make us unique—our differences lead us into adventure.

Before we begin the journey of learning how to live to give, we have to realize a few things about ourselves. We have to realize that each of us is truly unique. We each have unique passions and dreams. The boy in John 6 was one of a kind too. He was apparently the only one with a lunch that day. Mark 6:38 says that Jesus asked the disciples to "go and see" how many loaves were available. They must have looked pretty hard for bread in the crowd, thinking that surely several people would have thought to bring enough between them to throw together a quick potluck buffet. But no such luck. "When they found out," the Bible says, "they said [to Jesus], 'Five—and two fish.'" Really? One kid, out of all the five thousand-plus people, was the only one they found with a lunch?

You are unique as well, just like that kid, and so is *your* lunch. In order to learn how to live to give, you have to realize you are different from everyone else and embrace that. Each of us is a one-of-a-kind creation with different likes, dislikes, and taste buds. For instance, I like peanut butter on just about everything in the world. Seriously. Try it on a burger sometime. My extreme love of peanut butter is fairly distinctive to me and to my lunch. Each of us has different things that make us special in our own way. You are different—and that's a great thing! But the tricky part is believing that you truly are one of a kind and embracing the traits that make you that way. Easier said than done at times, I know.

Many times we attempt to fit into what we think of as the *normal* way to be. But I think being yourself is much cooler than being like everybody else. Call me crazy. Being yourself puts you under a lot less pressure too. And it can also be a lot of fun. Especially if your idea of fun is bungee jumping four hundred feet above the Zambezi River!

You're an original. Don't squash yourself into a cookie-cutter, *normal* mold. Join me in diving in to see what your uniqueness is all about.

Bunjee Jumping

YOUR FAVORITE LUNCH

What's your favorite food? Your favorite thing to eat for lunch? Is it mac and cheese? Pizza? A ham and peanut butter sandwich with pickles and a side of peanut butter? The funny thing about lunches is that, most of the time, they are very much our own. Whether you eat a packed lunch or order one from somewhere, your lunch is special. It is *your* lunch.

My mom packs my school lunch with different things from day to day, just to shake things up a little, but one thing usually stays the same. I normally include a little thing called an Uncrustable in my lunch. If you're not sure what an Uncrustable is, you should know that it is one of the greatest inventions in the history of mankind. Right up there with the lightbulb and Coke (and a few other things, of course). An Uncrustable starts out as a sandwich made of wonderful white bread with delicious, gooey peanut butter and jelly in the center. Then, the Smucker's people take an amazing, high-tech tool and press it onto the sandwich. The sandwich comes out smushed around the edges, becoming a nice peanut-buttery disk, and presto! No crust. Well, supposedly no crust . . .

Pretty incredible, isn't it?

Starting in my junior year of high school, I decided to bring two Uncrustables in my lunch every day because one just wouldn't do it for the growing teenager I had become. But I did something a little different with my Uncrustables. I wouldn't call it *weird*, but all my lunch buddies did. Every day I would take my Uncrustables and peel the crust off of them. Yes, it is called an Uncrustable for a reason, but it still has crust on it. Trust me. It just doesn't look like regular bread crust. (I firmly believe that I am not the only one who does this, so, for the sake of my sanity, please let me know if you do this too.) Every day my friends would remind me of the name of the sandwich, *Un-crust-able*. They also said the "crust" I thought was "crust" was really just bread. In the end, though, I would still peel that crust off of my Uncrustable and eat it the way I wanted to eat it. Why? The answer is simple: it fits my taste to pull off those edges—and it's my unique lunch, no one else's.

What would the world be like if, every day, everyone's lunch was exactly the same, and everyone ate it the very same way? Can you imagine that? From high school cafeterias to cafeterias in the corporate world to the McDonald's down the street, everyone would be having the same thing all the time. What if each of these places served only chicken sandwiches and soda? All of a sudden, the feeling of having something special and different would be gone. You walk into a Subway and ask for a number three, and what do you get? A chicken sandwich and a soda. You walk up to the hot dog stand

and it has a picture of a little chicken on the sign. It's like the world my dog, Bailey, lives in. She hasn't had much variety in her food for years; we give her the same kibbles every day. (She's still pretty happy about it, but she'd be overjoyed with the sloppiest, grossest leftovers every single day. Needless to say, she's easy to please.) But can you imagine if that were us? No variety, no uniqueness. It would get old pretty fast, and it wouldn't be long before eating wasn't fun anymore.

In school cafeterias, you get to show off the cool, special lunch you have. You always have something a little bit different from the person next to you.

Don't believe me? I have an experiment for you to try. The next time you bring your own lunch, look around. Walk through the cafeteria and look for someone who has the same exact lunch as you. If people start to look at you funny, just tell them to buy this book and they will understand.

> When God created us, He packed us each a lunch box with a different, delicious combination of spiritual "food."

I hate to give it all away, but if you do this experiment, you will find that almost nobody in the entire cafeteria has the same meal as you! In the same way, God has given each of us a special set of gifts. You could say that when

He created us, He packed each of us a lunch box with a different, delicious combination of spiritual "food." Have you ever thought about it like that? God didn't make it so that everyone always has a ham sandwich and a juice box; instead, He packed something special for you. But if you want to sit down and enjoy the lunch God put together for you, you have to start by accepting yourself and by being the person you are.

The stuff in your lunch is different from the person's next to you, and you should be glad about that. God hasn't given you the same gifts and talents as that person either, and that's also a good thing. God has made each of us different from one another in who we are, what our gifts and talents are, and even what we look like.

STUDY QUESTIONS

1. WHAT MAKES YOU DIFFERENT? NAME FIVE THINGS THAT MAKE YOU UNIQUE FROM THE PEOPLE YOU'RE AROUND ALL DAY.
2. HAS ANYONE EVER TOLD YOU THAT YOU HAVE A GIFT OR A TALENT? WHAT IS IT?
3. WHAT IS YOUR FAVORITE LUNCH? WHAT MIGHT THAT SAY ABOUT YOU?
4. HOW HAVE YOU BEEN TEMPTED TO SQUASH YOURSELF INTO SOMEONE ELSE'S MOLD IN THE PAST? IN WHAT WAYS DO YOU FACE PRESSURE TO BE THE SAME AS EVERYONE ELSE?
5. IN WHAT WAY CAN YOU EMBRACE YOUR DIFFERENTNESS THIS WEEK? HOW CAN YOU USE WHAT'S UNIQUELY YOURS TO HELP OR BLESS SOMEONE ELSE?

3

Different Outside and In

When God made you, He didn't pull out His gingerbread-man cookie cutter and cut you out of the same stuff as anyone else, or send you through the heavenly Uncrustables factory and stamp out another (delicious) sandwich just like the rest. David said in Psalm 139,

> You created my inmost being;
> you knit me together in my mother's womb.
> I praise you because I am fearfully and wonder-fully made. (vv. 13–14)

God made you by hand, and that means you're completely different from anybody else.

Did you know that even identical twins have different fingerprints?[1] Just goes to show that even though there are people who may seem the same on the outside, God hasn't made any two of us completely alike.

You've probably realized that no one else looks just like you, even if you're not exactly in love with what you look like. You may resemble a few people in your family or other kids at school, but they don't look *exactly* like you. Unless, of course, you are an identical twin, in which case we'd have to look at your fingerprints, but that's pretty cool in itself.

Have you ever wanted to change a few things about your appearance? Ever thought maybe God got a couple of things wrong? You're not alone. I feel that way too sometimes. It's important to remember, though, that there are entire industries that sell cosmetics, fitness products, clothing, and other things meant to "improve" your appearance, and they pay good money to advertising companies so they can make you feel bad enough about the way you look that you'll go out and buy what they're selling. Just crack open a magazine or turn on the TV, and you'll be instantly hit with an assortment of messages and images that are designed to make you feel not buff enough, not thin enough, not stylish enough, or not good-looking enough. But even if you watch out for those advertisements and try to guard against them, it's human nature to think that the grass is greener on the other side, or that other people have it better than you in the looks department. We look at the people around us and compare ourselves to them. It makes us feel uncomfortable, unsafe to be different from everyone else.

I'm no exception. Through the years, I have had a pretty long list of things I wished I could change about my appearance. When I was younger, I was short. I'm not talking short like I just hadn't grown into my shoes yet—I mean really short. I think I was hovering somewhere around 4'11" to 5'1" for far too long, about a head under the other kids my age. It wasn't until I started the tenth grade that I really started to grow.

I also didn't like that I had freckles. I don't know why, but they sometimes bothered me. I didn't like that when I went outside, even for a few minutes, I didn't tan—I burned. And not like a regular sunburn. Imagine a strawberry. That was me after going outside, except I was a 4'11" strawberry in a T-shirt. Don't forget, though, that my hair has a nice tint of red and blond to it; they call it "strawberry blond." Appropriate for a 4'11" strawberry, don't you think?

Does my list sound a little too long? These are all things that I didn't like about myself at times. Some of these things I don't really like today. But does that list sound exactly like yours? Probably not. And the reason is that God has made you different from me. We look different—we *are* different—and that is actually a good thing.

I am learning to be happy about who God created me to be because, in the end, I am who God wants me to be. Do you believe that? I would encourage you to dwell on Genesis 1:27: "So God created mankind in his own image, in the image of God he created them; male and female he created them."

God has created *you* to look just like Him. We are made in the image of the Creator of the universe. What an amazing thing! We are made just like Him. We don't have to compare ourselves to the people on TV or in magazines or even people we come into contact with on the street. We don't need to poke and prod and pound ourselves into something we're not when we're already made in the image of the God, who made the whole world!

The next time you or I think about the things we don't like about ourselves, let's try to remember this verse, that we are created in the image of God. Let's pray for God to help us have a good, healthy appreciation of the faces and bodies He's given us. We all know that what's on the outside isn't everything, but the way you look is part of the individuality God gave you. What an incredible thing to know we have a family resemblance with Him (though I don't think God gets sunburned!).

ONE-OF-A-KIND PERSONALITY

There are probably small character flaws or bad habits that we should change about ourselves on the inside, and God will help us deal with those as we grow in Him. But aside from the harmful things that God wants to transform for us, we should be happy with who God created us to be, outside *and* inside. Are you a little shy? There is nothing wrong with that. Are you the class clown? I sure wasn't. In my family, my sister and my dad are the ones who have the gift of comedy. They know how to make the whole family belly-laugh so hard it hurts. My sister can randomly start quoting lines from our favorite movie, *Nacho Libre*, and create a perfect, hilarious moment. (I am a firm believer that this movie, along with a Bible and a copy of the Constitution, should be required in all households.) I never had that gift, and I secretly wish I did. But it just isn't my personality, and that's okay! God gave me other gifts. And, as it turns out, people tell me they actually think it's funny when I try to make a joke that totally isn't funny! Who knew? (They're laughing *with* me, right?)

You might not believe it, but the gifts, talents, and personality traits you have are truly amazing. God gave them to you, and He delights in you! So embrace that knowledge and do not look down on the talents you've been given. They are remarkable and specially designed just for you. God purposefully made a wonderful person in you, so don't feel bad about accepting that. Just as Genesis 1:27 describes your resemblance to God, your gifts and talents reflect who He is too. You look like the Creator of the universe inside and out.

The Bible tells us, "What marvelous love the Father has extended to us! Just look at it—we're called children of God! That's who we really are" (1 John 3:1 MSG). Just as a kid might have his mom's nose or his dad's knees or his grandmother's sense of humor, we reflect our amazing Father in completely individual ways. We represent

> You look like the Creator of the universe inside and out.

who He is. And you have to admit, He's pretty amazing. For instance, a friend of mine has her granddad's red hair. Whenever someone gives her a compliment (or even makes some kind of rude comment) on her red hair, she always thinks of her granddad, how much she loves him and he loves her, and smiles. She resembles him, and that's a gift no matter what!

So when you open the lunch God packed for you and see a personality or appearance that you might not have chosen for yourself, you can relax and know that the gifts God put there are made from the very best ingredients, handpicked by Him from His very own supply.

SPIRITUAL GIFTS

What God has given you in your lunch box is so perfect and unique to you, it is almost unbelievable. And what are those incredible gifts and talents? We will explore this more in depth soon, but for now think about what you're good at. Maybe you are smart, maybe you are a good encourager, or maybe you are naturally an amazing basketball player. If something comes easily to you, people might call you *gifted* at that thing. But the Bible covers a few specific gifts called *spiritual gifts* or *gifts of the spirit*. Paul talked about them in 1 Corinthians, and he listed a few as examples. He said,

> All kinds of things are handed out by the Spirit, and to all kinds of people! The variety is wonderful:
>
> > wise counsel
> > clear understanding
> > simple trust
> > healing the sick
> > miraculous acts
> > proclamation
> > distinguishing between spirits
> > tongues
> > interpretation of tongues.

All these gifts have a common origin, but are handed out one by one by the one Spirit of God. He decides who gets what, and when. (12:7–11 MSG)

But that's not all. Paul wrote about some more gifts in Romans 12:6–11:

We have different gifts, according to the grace given to each of us. If your gift is *prophesying*, then prophesy in accordance with your faith; if it is *serving*, then serve; if it is *teaching*, then teach; if it is to *encourage*, then give encouragement; if it is *giving*, then give generously; if it is to *lead*, do it diligently; if it is to show *mercy*, do it cheerfully. (emphasis added)

Does any of that sound familiar to you? Does anything sound like something in your lunch box? Some of these gifts are pretty easy to understand (like "wise counsel") and some are a little more complicated. If you're wondering about these spiritual gifts, what they are, and which ones you might be gifted with, talk to your pastor, parents, or youth minister, or check out some of the many books and online resources available to people who want to learn what their gifts are and how to use them. There are all sorts of tools, tests, and quizzes that can help you discover your gifts in a way that is tailored to your distinct personality.[2]

I believe any talent can be a spiritual gift—not just the ones in Paul's list above. If you live to give and offer your gift to God just as our friend offered his lunch to Jesus, consider it spiritual! It doesn't even have to be a super impressive or well-developed gift (like opera singing or Olympic diving) to be useful to God. For instance, I really, really love the game of basketball. Shooting hoops with my dad is one of my favorite things to do in the whole world, and there is nothing I like better than watching the Phoenix Suns occasionally beat the Los Angeles Lakers (or any team, for that matter). I love the sound of a swish because, for me, it is a rarer occurrence than it might be for others. A swish for me is like hearing that song on the radio I really like and always wanting the station to play it again.

I always wanted to be a great basketball player. I could picture myself dunking or hitting a free throw once in a while. The funny thing is, I'm just not naturally talented at it. Yep, it's true. Even though I started a basketball-based charity, basketball doesn't come naturally to me. Plus, with the whole 4'11" thing that went on for so long, I was kept off most NBA draft lists. That doesn't mean I don't try or that I don't love the game; I just realize that God has gifted me in different areas. But when God got hold of my fair-to-medium basketball abilities, He turned them into something He could use, even though my free-throw percentage is nowhere close to perfect! He knew I loved it, and He used it.

What do you love to do? Do you love reading? Taking care of animals? Rock climbing? Drawing? Hiking? Talking to people? God put that desire, interest, or passion in your heart, and He can use that and your other spiritual gifts to do amazing things. The areas God has gifted you in are very special. You are an incredible person no matter what you are good at or what your spiritual gifts are. Be thankful that God has gifted you in the ways He has.

We are all different in so many ways—in who we are, what we look like, and what our lunch boxes are full of. Let's thank Him every day for making us that way!

GIFT ENVY

So you are different from the person next to you. Does that mean your spiritual gifts aren't as important as the person's next to you? No, not at all. Your gifts aren't *better*, but they aren't worse either. You see, it goes back to the example of how boring it would be if we all had to eat the same lunch every day. No lunch is greater than another, and they all are needed to fulfill God's will.

One thing I love is humor in the Bible. And believe me, there's humor in there. Ever heard the story of

Balaam and the talking donkey (Numbers 22:21–34)? Now that's a pretty funny image. Someone might say that Bible humor is corny, but I say it's funny. Talking donkeys scaring the pants off their owners—that's pretty good. Paul spiced up his letter about spiritual gifts with some humor when he talked about this issue of whether one gift is better than another. Let's look at a few foundational (unfunny) verses that really show what Paul was saying.

First, starting in 1 Corinthians 12:12, Paul talked about the fact that there are many parts of a body. Here is what he said: "Just as a body, though one, has many parts, but all its many parts form one body, so it is with Christ."

We don't have just one big "body"; we have many parts that make up our bodies—elbows and nostrils and such. That's how God made the church too. He has made each one of us with unique gifts and talents that come together to make up a living, moving, growing body of Christ.

Next, in verses 13 and 14, Paul talked about the fact that we all are one in Christ:

For we were all baptized by one Spirit so as to form one body—whether Jews or Gentiles, slave or free—and we were all given the one Spirit to drink. Even so the body is not made up of one part but of many.

If we are followers of Christ, we are one. It doesn't matter if you are black, white, yellow, or green. It doesn't matter if you are a butcher, a baker, or a candlestick maker. It is very important to understand that as brothers and sisters in Christ, we all work together to do God's will. We all are God's children. Together we make up the body of Christ.

In verses 15–17, Paul started to speak with the biblical humor I have grown so fond of. Look at what he said here.

> Now if the foot should say, "Because I am not a hand, I do not belong to the body," it would not for that reason stop being part of the body. And if the ear should say, "Because I am not an eye, I do not belong to the body," it would not for that reason stop being part of the body. If the whole body were an eye, where would the sense of hearing be? If the whole body were an ear, where would the sense of smell be?

Ha! Can you imagine your foot saying to you, "I'm not important enough and I don't belong as a part of your body," and then running off on its own? You would probably first ask your foot how it can speak, and then tell your foot that it is *absolutely* valued. You need your foot to walk every day, so you'd better be pretty nice to it if it complains. If your whole body were an eye, Paul asked, where would your sense of smell be? A whole body being an eye . . . I don't know what that would look like, but it would definitely be pretty scary.

I am so glad that God didn't make all of us huge, frightening eyeballs like Paul said. That part of the passage is my favorite. Can you imagine a giant nose teaching your classes, or big, people-sized feet hopping around the halls of your school? Sure, the mental image of a body made of a foot or eye is weirdly funny, but I love Paul's message behind it too.

Have you ever felt like you aren't valuable enough because God hasn't given you the same spiritual gifts as the person next to you? Because He hasn't made you good at the same things? On the other hand, have you ever looked down on someone because they don't have the same spiritual gifts that you have? If each and every one of us in the church were gifted in the area of preaching, how would the money be handled? Who would make sure the electric bill got paid? We'd all be sitting there every Sunday in the dark. You need an accountant or someone else at a church to take care of those important things, but then you also need a pastor. The church can't run without either person, and thus, neither is more valuable than another. Sure, the pastor may be the most visible person in the church, but you also need the many different people who work together to make the place function.

Now think about your local sit-down restaurant. (As you may be able to tell, I love food.) In a restaurant, you don't just have a cook making your food; you have many different people at work to make the restaurant run. When you first walk in, you see a host or hostess who seats you. Then you have a server. Next, the chef makes your meal for you. As you leave, a busboy clears the table for the next guest. All these people work together to make up the restaurant experience, and that's not even counting the farmers who grow the food, the carpenters who make the tables, and the plumbers who put in the restrooms. Without one of these people, the restaurant could fall apart.

In the same way, we are each a part of the body of Christ, each with an important role. In verse 19, Paul reiterated the idea that a body cannot be one part: "If they were all one part, where would the body be? As it is, there are many parts, but one body."

I don't want us to forget what happens starting with verse 22, though. I love this part of the passage because what Paul said in this section really hits home to me. He was talking about those parts of the body that we think might be not worth much: "On the contrary, those parts of the body that seem to be *weaker* are *indispensable*" (emphasis added).

As we saw when we were talking about the church and the restaurant, we might think that one person is weaker or less valuable than another, but in reality that person is so valuable that the body of Christ wouldn't be able to function without him or her.

Author Andy Andrews writes a lot about something called the "butterfly effect." It's based on the idea that when a butterfly flaps its wings, it could cause a hurricane over on the other side of the world. Wild, right? People, he says, are like butterflies flapping their wings. Even if the littlest, most insignificant person does one thing to make a difference, who knows how it could turn out? For instance, he tells the story of a farmer in Missouri a long time ago who took in a tiny orphaned slave child and decided to raise him. That child grew up to be George Washington Carver, a brilliant scientist who came up with hundreds of uses for the peanut and sweet potato. Carver set in motion a chain of events that eventually led to a man named Norman Borlaug inventing a kind of corn that saved two billion people from starvation. *Two billion people.* All from one farmer, who showed mercy to a little baby.[3] Even the most seemingly small things make a huge difference!

Paul wrapped up his discussion of the way we should treat the weak with something important in verses 23–25:

And the parts that we think are less honorable we treat with special honor . . . while our presentable parts need no special treatment. But God has put the body together, giving greater honor to the parts that lacked it, so that there should be no division in the body, but that its parts should have equal concern for each other.

Wow—that goes against the grain, doesn't it? Paul basically said that we should treat those parts that *don't* seem to have much value as if they had even *more* value. Those little seemingly insignificant parts can have a huge butterfly effect for God. The parts that are clearly, obviously valuable don't need to be shown that they are valuable. Sure, value them, let them do their thing, but don't shower them with extra honor and praise. It's more important to show those behind the scenes that they are valuable, because they might forget. How gracious is that message?

Paul closed with saying that by doing these things we can have "equal concern for each other." If you are up front and in the spotlight, I encourage you to live out this instruction. Whether you are the class president, the captain of the football team, or just an all-around visible person, highlight those who aren't always highlighted. Make them feel special in front of everyone else, because you wouldn't be able to function the same way without them. When a less visible person gives support, everyone feels the benefit. But if the seemingly tiny thing that person takes care of doesn't get done, things could go south—fast! Small things can in fact make a huge difference. Take this story, for instance:

> Not long ago there was a wreck on the Southern Pacific [Railway]. Investigation showed that a track, supposed to be solid, had been undermined by a squirrel, the hole had left a place for water to gather, the roadbed had become soft. Along came a heavy train and it was plunged to destruction; all because of a trifle, the vagrant meandering of a mite. It is not given to all to deal directly with big things, but the one who deals with small things has a mission as important.[4]

So, after all this, if you're still secretly wondering whether one spiritual gift is better than another, we can now confirm that the Bible's answer is no. If you are secretly wishing you had someone else's gift because it seems fancier, take a step back and read these passages from 1 Corinthians again. Let them soak in and renew your heart, and then start getting excited. Paul said it pretty clearly: *Your* gift is special. It is useful. If you ever feel like you don't have as much value as another one of God's followers, know that you do. The body of Christ wouldn't be able to function without you. And you can't function without that person next to you. The body of Christ needs all its parts to be able to run, jump, dance, and do all the things it was meant to do!

LIVING TO GIVE

Ethel is from Zambia and works in one of the clinics Hoops of Hope built. Every day she gives injections, wipes noses, and helps people with injuries and those who are dying of Africa's most dreaded disease, AIDS. She also has a gift and a passion for administration and hard work, and she has a real talent for nursing and caring for people. She is good at these things, and she blesses many people by using her gifts. I met Ethel in Zambia in May of 2011 when I traveled there with my dad and a few service volunteers from Intel Corporation. One day we all decided to go and make an unscheduled visit to a clinic that Hoops of Hope had built a year earlier. We honestly didn't know what to expect, but when we got there, we were blown away.

Ethel was surprised by our visit but happy to show us around. She showed us the full waiting area, with more than fifty people waiting to be tested and treated for HIV/AIDS. She showed us how these people were tested. She talked about the process and how she and the staff at the clinic would counsel them. She and only two other people did all of this.

What makes this so incredible is that in the eleven

Clinic Waiting Room

months the clinic has been open, over a thousand people's lives have been saved because of the work Ethel and her colleagues have done. A thousand people!

We also met a mom with two kids at the clinic. The father had died of AIDS, but the mom was alive and able to take care of her children because of this clinic and Ethel's care. Otherwise, she would have died, and her children would have been AIDS orphans, unable to take care of themselves and living every day in danger. All these people were saved because Ethel uses her gifts.

What if Ethel had decided to do something else? What if she had gotten down on herself and started thinking that nursing wasn't as cool or as important as other jobs, and had gone off to try other, more glamorous or flashy things? Nursing can be hard, heartbreaking work, and it isn't that easy to find another nurse willing to move to a rural village to provide HIV/AIDS testing, but Ethel does this work on a daily basis. She is using what is unique in her lunch to save lives. That is what it is all about.

•••••◆•••••

God has given you the unique lunch you have for a purpose. Remember the boy who had a pretty unique lunch of his own? Starting in John 6:9 we find out that he had a lunch of "five small barley loaves and two small fish." Thought I was odd for peeling the crust off of my Uncrustable? The boy's lunch might look pretty weird at the lunch table at your school (how would he cook those fish?). He may have left home that morning wishing he had a falafel wrap instead, or something fancy like the kid down the street usually brought. The lunch might not have been what the people in the crowd would have preferred if they'd been able to pick what was on the menu that day. But in the end, it was the best lunch ever. Jesus didn't turn up His nose at this boy's basic meal. Instead, He used it to do one of the most incredible miracles this world has ever seen.

Even if God didn't give you what you thought you wanted, trust me—He gave you the perfect lunch. What a great thing to know that the Creator of the universe values you so much! You have the perfect lunch. You have the best lunch. And guess what? The person next to you has the best lunch too.

Being a part of Team Christ is an amazing adventure, and it illustrates what teamwork is all about. Together, when we each bring the lunch we have, we make up that team. Nothing is better or more fulfilling than seeing the miraculous things He brings about.

STUDY QUESTIONS

1. What is unique about your lunch?
2. What do you like about being different, both inside and out? Make a list.
3. How do you think you can use your uniqueness as a gift to the world in a larger way?
4. Have you ever wished you weren't unique? When? Looking back, why did you think that?
5. What is it like to know that there is nobody as *you* as you are?

4

What's in Your Lunch Box?

I know you're dying to know: *How exactly do I know what is in my lunch box? How do I know what these spiritual gifts are that God has given me?* By now you may have a bit of an idea about what your spiritual gifts are. Finding the answers to these questions may be a lot easier for some than others. With God's help, though, it can be as easy as opening a lunch box. There isn't just one way to go about discovering your spiritual gifts. I'm going to tell you about three good ways, and there are more. Let's start by going straight to the source of your lunch.

ASK YOUR MAKER

The first and most direct way to discover what God has given you is just to ask Him. Simple as that. The Bible says, "Ask and it will be given to you; seek and you will find; knock and the door will be opened to you" (Matthew 7:7). So rest assured, if you keep asking and praying, God will reveal your gifts to you and answer the prayers you pray. He promises, "I will do whatever you ask in my name, so that the Father may be glorified in the Son" (John 14:13). So ask! Remember, God put your gifts in your lunch box for you in the first place, so why not go straight to the source?

As we said before, your gifts are something altogether special. They don't look like the ones God gave anyone else. Something tells me He is just as happy to tell us about our gifts as we are to hear it!

LOOK IN THE MIRROR

The second way to find out what your spiritual gifts are is to simply look at your own life. What do you like to do? What gets you pumped up and passionate? What pulls your heartstrings or makes you cry? What's an activity you could do for hours on end? Part of being unique is having different likes and wants. Just as everyone does not want the same thing for lunch, you have different tastes and preferences in what's important to you as well. I love basketball. I might not be great, maybe not even good, but I enjoy it, and it's still one of my favorite things to do. So God used it! Use what God has given you. Those likes and tastes of yours can be used to make a huge impact.

I've seen this in action in the life of a girl named Amber Landas. Amber wanted to be a part of Hoops of Hope, but she wasn't really into basketball. I can't sympathize, but I guess we're all different! Amber had a passion for helping others in need, and she decided to do it in an unconventional way. You see, Amber is good at knitting. Kitting is one of the special things God packed in Amber's lunch. So Amber decided to knit blankets to help others. Amber enjoys knitting and likes to do it for fun—and she took it to the next level by using it to change lives. She knitted several blankets and sent them to our house a

Blankets in Zambia

few weeks before we were to leave for Africa in June 2010. We were headed to Zambia again to visit an AIDS testing clinic that was about to open. We made room for those blankets in our suitcases and flew them across the ocean with us. When we got there, we passed them on to new mothers at one of the clinics that Hoops of Hope had built. We couldn't believe what an incredible impact those blankets had. For us, a new blanket might not be too big of a deal, but for many of those mothers, it was the first blanket they had ever had. It would keep them and their babies warm for years to come. All because Amber knew what she liked to do and offered it to God. And she made a world of a difference.

ASK SOMEONE MORE "EXPERIENCED"

If we're lucky, we have several adults in our lives who love us and have taken on the job of looking out for us—spiritually, physically, and emotionally. I'm talking about our parents, caregivers, and pastors at church. They usually know us pretty well, and they might have some observations to give us. Plus, they've been around awhile and might know one or two useful things about life in general. Who am I kidding? They're gold mines!

Parents

We've been talking about how God packs our spiritual

lunch boxes with special, hand-selected gifts and talents. But as far as real-life lunches go, in many cases, your parents get the job of helping to pack them for school (especially when you were too small to reach the cupboards or slap a sandwich together). Think about it. Do you pack your lunch, or does your mom or someone else? My mom packs my lunch most of the time. She always has it set out on the counter ready for me to take. Sometimes it even has my name on it. She's a pretty nice lady. My mom takes care of me and loves to feed me, so she takes responsibility for packing my lunch.

Do you think the boy in the book of John had a mom who packed bread and fish for his lunch? The Bible doesn't give many details about him, but if his mom was anything like mine, the boy probably didn't pack his own food. He probably had a mother behind the scenes who helped him. (Just think how proud she would have been after hearing how many people got to sample her baking that day!)

In the same way, parents have the ability to help pack the spiritual lunch for their child. It is more than just the ability, though; it is a privilege. Parents have a one-of-a-kind chance to spur on a child's likes and interests.

Hoops of Hope never would have existed if it were not for my parents' encouragement and support. When I told my dad how my heart hurt for the orphan Maggie in the video we watched together, he believed in me enough to point me in the right direction and toward the right people. He might not have thought anything was going to come of it, but he never squashed my dreams or made me feel like I was too young or couldn't make a difference. Same for my mom. From the time I was very young, my parents built up my passion by helping me make a difference. For instance, they supported my passion for the homeless.

When I was younger, the suffering of homeless people always touched my heart. Every time I'd walk by a guy who was begging on the street, I'd want to give him anything I had. I was floored by the simple thought of someone being so poor and needy that he would be willing to literally beg someone for money. But did I have five bucks to give the man? No—I was just a kid. My parents did, though, and their giving taught me to give. Their giving taught me that it is good to care, and that giving is one of the greatest things I could do.

How can our parents help us find out what our spiritual gifts are? Let this question be the start of a good conversation. Our parents are in a special position to bring out our gifts and talents by helping us, their kids, pinpoint our passions. They pack our lunches, so to speak, and they have perspective on our personalities. So ask them! Ask for their guidance.

I realize not everyone is as fortunate as I am in the parent department. If you don't have parents in your life you can talk to, I'd really encourage you to talk to another responsible adult you have a lot of respect for. A grandparent? An aunt, uncle, teacher, or maybe a leader or adult from your church? Find someone who is using his or her gifts and who knows and loves you enough to help you discover yours. Here are some great questions to ask them:

1. What do you see me being passionate about?
2. What do you see as my likes and interests?
3. What do you see me doing around the house or in my spare time that I really enjoy?

If a child loves kicking around a soccer ball or watching games, parents can encourage her interest in soccer. They can help her pursue her passion. And if parents help that kid get involved with a soccer league and make sure she stays involved, a passion can turn into a real skill! Soccer can be a spiritual gift from God, and it can be used to serve God.

Your gift doesn't even have to be sports! My sister, Brittany, is an amazing person. She is only fourteen months younger than I am, and she is my best friend. Brittany is also an incredible artist and drummer. My parents encourage these things, and now she is using her passion for art to inspire people. As my great-grandmother was passing away this past summer, I remember seeing her eyes light up at Britt's art. When it comes to drums, my sister is starting to play for the high school ministry at our church. Whatever you are passionate about can make a huge difference—especially with support. I am so proud of my sister and the way she makes an impact on the world around her!

Parents can encourage a child's passions, but they also have the task of showing him or her how to give and serve. Another way a parent can spur on a child is through outreach. Why not ask your parents to show you how they serve? Maybe you can all go down to a rescue mission and serve for a morning. Or find some other way to give to those in need. Pointing the way toward service opportunities helps kids find out what breaks their hearts, and that's just as important as figuring out what they're passionate about. Why? Because, as a good friend taught me at the beginning of Hoops of Hope, if you combine what breaks your heart and what you are passionate about, you can change the world for God. So ask for your parents' support and perspective today—you never know what kind of great insight you'll find!

Youth Pastors and Churches

Your church isn't just the "body of Christ"; they're part of your family—your spiritual family. And, like your parents, your pastors have something special to contribute to helping you find out what your spiritual gifts are. There is nothing better than the encouragement of a youth pastor. He or she can really help you when it comes to finding out what is in your lunch box, and what it might look like to start to give it to God. This is also the responsibility of the children's pastor and even the senior pastor of a church.

I have always loved being around youth pastors and children's pastors. They have such great knowledge of God, and they care about kids like nobody else. When I was nine years old and just figuring out the first few steps toward Hoops of Hope, I really loved having the support of my children's pastor. I had my family behind me too, but it meant so much to have support from people I looked up to that way.

When I first started, a guy named Chris Hedrick was my children's pastor. He loved what I was doing and wanted to get everyone involved. Then there was Nathan Maples, a man who poured his time, heart, and energy into my life. I loved and respected him. He did his best to make sure everyone in our youth group was doing Hoops of Hope and everyone was involved in some way, year after year. Nathan also had me share the message in the youth group many times. But he also cared a lot about me and my passion. To this day, Nathan still encourages me in everything I do, showing me that the gifts I think I might have are real, and that they really can be useful. There are many other adults who have helped me make a difference, and they have had a huge impact on my life and the lives of others.

So how can your pastors help you find out what's in your particular lunch box? Set up a meeting or give them a call. Tell them that you're interested in finding out what your gifts are, and that you're ready and willing to use them for God's glory. Tell them what you've been reading about and explore these things together:

1. What you're passionate about
2. The things that break your heart
3. The ways you want to serve God
4. What you're praying and dreaming about, and what God has led you toward so far

Then ask for their encouragement and perspective. Ask for ideas, and especially for prayer. It could be the start of an awesome journey together.

The Impact of Adults

I know there are many kids who are amped up and ready to go, and they really want to make a difference. Sometimes I get e-mails from kids telling me they have discovered something they are passionate about, but they've been told there is too much going on in their churches already. In one particular instance, a youth pastor said that they didn't need "another canned food drive." What could be wrong with another canned food drive? I wonder. Was there no other way to help this kid bring in food for the hungry? Unfortunately, these dreams weren't met with a "yes" but rather an "I'm sorry."

The youth workers and parents of the world play such a huge role in helping kids make a difference. If you have an influence on the youth, this is for you.

Dear parents, youth workers, and everyday heroes,

Every time you say yes to a child or to a child's dream, you are having an impact. You are having an impact larger than you'll ever know. You may never know how big a story God is going to write through that child, and it all can start because you say yes. To have an impact, say yes. Be the parent or children's pastor or youth pastor who says yes to their dreams. Be the one who encourages them like none other. And never have doubts as to whether or not you are having an impact. You *are*.

A ROCK IN HIS LUNCHBOX

There once was a boy who had one of the greatest impacts in the history of the world. I think he was pretty cool. He faced danger, but he didn't think armor was necessary. He was up against a mighty power, but he didn't think army formations were very effective. He didn't let the shadow of the ten-foot problem bog him down. He didn't let doubts stand in the way. He let a stone fly. He let his dream fly. He killed a ten-foot giant of a problem with a tiny, insignificant stone.

This is a story I am sure that many of us could recite pretty well. (If you aren't familiar with it, read 1 Samuel 17.) It is the story of a kid who wanted to stand up and use his gifts to face a problem, and he wasn't stopped by the youth pastor or his parents standing on the sidelines. It's a story that tells of a turning point for a nation. That young boy, David, grew up to lead that nation. Imagine if those adults on the sidelines had stopped him.

My encouragement to parents and youth pastors alike is that there are Davids around you. You have the chance to encourage them. You have the chance to help them open their lunches and have an impact for God. When you say yes to their dreams, you might be saying yes to God. Remember, the God who lives, breathes, and speaks to adults is the *exact* same God who lives, breathes, and speaks to children who know and love Him. Plus, imagine if you were the one who first helped David discover he was pretty good with a rock and a slingshot!

My encouragement to those trying to figure out what their spiritual gifts are is to pray and search diligently, but know there is a David inside of you. You can change the world. So pick up your stone and let it fly.

STUDY QUESTIONS

1. WHAT IS YOUR PASSION? WHAT DO YOU LIKE TO DO?
2. WHOM DO YOU FEEL PASSIONATE ABOUT HELPING?
3. WHAT BREAKS YOUR HEART?
4. WHAT IS HOLDING YOU BACK FROM LETTING THAT STONE FLY?
5. WHICH ADULTS IN YOUR LIFE WHO WOULD BE GOOD SOURCES FOR INSIGHT? HOW CAN YOU START A CONVERSATION WITH THEM THIS WEEK?

5

Don't Lose Your Lunch!

We talked about how David overcame the fact that he was just a kid and had the confidence to use his gift. There must have been plenty of other discouraging factors that could have gotten him down (a huge, taunting, smelly giant, for instance). But I love David's story because he didn't let anything get to him. Once you pop open your lunch box and start to dig through it to see what's inside, you might notice some factors around you that could distract or discourage you from giving your spiritual gifts to God. But you, like David, have what it takes to kick those things to the curb. You're on God's team, and He's got the muscle! All you have to do is be aware.

If you're just finding out about your spiritual gifts, good for you! With the help of God, some self-reflection, and people who love you, you'll soon be rocking and rolling and living to give. Before we go on, though, we should talk about a few things to look out for so that process can continue. Let me take you back to the school cafeteria for a moment to start us off.

JUNK FOOD

As I said before, lunchtime is always one of the best times of the day. You will notice many things in the hustle and bustle of the cafeteria. One of the things I notice is the kid who always has the best lunch. You know the one I'm talking about. The kid with all that food your parents tell you not to eat too much of. The one whose lunch bag looks like the snack bar at the movie theater. I am not talking about the best lunch as in the most nutritious, but the best lunch as in the one everyone craves. I'm sure you can always spot that kid at the lunch table. Maybe you are that kid! Or maybe you are one of the rest of us who look on as he eats, your mouth watering, craving that delicious lunch. It may look something like this: pizza rolls, a Slim Jim, a Coke, and, of course, a Twinkie—maybe even a chocolate Twinkie. Like I said, not necessarily the most nutritious meal we have ever seen. Nothing in that kid's bag grew out of the ground or came from the organic section of the grocery store. But, man, does it look good.

What is it about that lunch? It looks great on the outside, but if you read the nutrition label on that Twinkie package, you'd realize they never really did him any good on the inside. The interesting thing about each of those items that I listed is they are, for the most part, man-made. There is no Slim Jim tree or Coke waterfall (though wouldn't it be awesome if there were?). No, these junk foods are a good symbol for the things mankind makes up, the things of the world that may fill us up and make us feel good for a little while but have no lasting nutritional value. What happens when you fill up on what the world gives you? You get hungry easier, your teeth rot out, and eventually you get sick! And what happens when you fill up on what God gives you? You grow strong and healthy.

Isn't it true that the things that are not from God are often more appealing? Flashier, more glamorous looking, more exciting? Or more covered in whipped cream and peanut butter? Trust me, I am not saying I am a healthy eater, by any means. I suffer from a long-term, incurable craving for Taco Bell. Those chalupas are amazing. But I do believe there is a life lesson to be learned from junk food. When it comes to finding out our gifts and our talents, we have a choice between seeking out what God wants us to do and what the world wants us to do. Life is a constant battle between choosing God and choosing the world—between what He put in your lunch and cravable, ultimately unsatisfying snacks. So in order to keep our eyes open, our hearts focused, and to determine the right choice, let's look at one of the first choices ever made.

THE CHOICE BETWEEN TWO TREES

Most of us know the story of Adam and Eve and the fall of mankind, but I think the life lessons found in it are worth going through again. When God put Adam and Eve in the garden of Eden and made them the world's first caretakers, He gave them the run of the place. There was only one rule: don't eat from one particular tree in the center of the garden. Everything else was fair game. In Genesis 3:1, the Bible says:

> Now the serpent was more crafty than any of the wild animals the Lord God had made. He said to the woman, "Did God really say, 'You must not eat from any tree in the garden'?"

The serpent, better known as Satan, our enemy, posed an interesting question here. He made Eve think, *Did God really say that?* I'd say she knew pretty clearly what God meant when He told them to stay away; after all, she and Adam had not eaten from the tree up until then. She reminded the serpent,

> We may eat fruit from the trees in the garden, but God did say, "You must not eat fruit from the tree that is in the middle of the garden, and you must not touch it, or you will die." (vv. 2–3)

Eve realized that God was up front and serious about not eating from this tree. It was full of the worst kind of junk food. Plus, she knew she was allowed to eat from every other tree in the garden. Can you imagine that? Waking up in paradise and thinking, *Hmm . . . What do I want today? A little mango, some kiwi, an apple, an orange, maybe some of that God-made chalupa tree?* She had all the trees in the garden. She could have whatever she wanted, just not anything from that one tree. But, as the story goes, the serpent's question made her doubt, made her think about that forbidden fruit in a new way, and she started to develop a craving.

Doesn't this tell us something true in our lives today? I know in my head that I have so much, but often the thing I don't have is the thing I want the most. Do you find yourself craving those things that you don't have? That game system, those designer jeans, that awesome jeep, that ability to run a five-minute mile? We really have everything we could ever need. God takes care of us, and He always provides. Sometimes, though, it is harder to choose what God gave us. This is not to say that we shouldn't try to learn and grow in God, to become more like Jesus, or to have goals and aspirations. But we do need to look carefully at what it is we're going after and decide whether or not it is junk food.

We all know how the story of the fall ends: Adam and Eve eat the fruit and sin comes into the world. But really, the end of their story is the beginning of ours. If Adam and Eve hadn't eaten the fruit, if we weren't all sinners, Christ would not have had to die for you and me to save us from the sin in our hearts and from the unhealthy things we crave.

There are two lessons I want to pull from this story—two really important things we can learn from Adam and Eve. The first is about being content with what we have, and the second is about the lies we'll come up against as we seek to use our spiritual gifts.

Using our gifts won't necessarily always be easy, but it is worth it. Professional surfer Bethany Hamilton is an awesome example of someone who continues to use her gifts in spite of what most would consider an insurmountable challenge. At the age of thirteen, she

DON'T LOSE YOUR LUNCH!

lost her arm in a tragic shark attack, but that didn't stop her from getting back on her board. Today, she surfs professionally, and her story has inspired millions.

Like Adam and Eve, we have choices to make. We can make the right ones with God's help and the help of our spiritual families. Just as we're never too young to make a difference, we're also never too young to make good decisions about the use of our gifts. So let's explore these lessons and start to exercise our choice-making muscles.

CHOOSING TO BE SATISFIED

We've already talked about appreciating your uniqueness, about learning to love the ways God made you different. Now let's talk about being content and maintaining that attitude for the long term. The Bible says, "Your enemy the devil prowls around like a roaring lion looking for someone to devour" (1 Peter 5:8). That serpent is *still* trying to eat your lunch. He's doing everything he can to get you to let go of it, even to the point of tempting you and making you dissatisfied with your own gifts so you'll run after something else besides God. It's slimy, but true.

For example, think about the physical things we have. If you are reading this book in America, I want to ask you a few tough questions: What did you do to be born here? Why are you here? Did you have control over that? These were questions I asked myself many times while I was thinking about the orphan Maggie's story. What made her and me so different? Why was she born into poverty while I was born into riches by the world's standards?

My family isn't necessarily wealthy by America's standards, but by the world's we are. Did you know that if you get twenty bucks a week for your allowance you are in the top 42 percent of the world's richest people?[1] If you have a reasonable job and are making $100 a week, you are in the top 14 percent of the world. Did you also know that $8 could buy you fifteen organic apples in America or twenty-five whole fruit trees for farmers in Honduras? Or how about the fact that $73 could buy you a new cell phone or buy a new mobile health clinic for children in Uganda?[2]

The reason why I ask these challenging questions is to help you think. You should not feel guilty for being born in America or being wealthy. You're blessed! God put you here. The cool thing is that we get to choose to do something with all this wealth. It's part of living to give. Jesus said it Himself in Luke 12:48: "From everyone who has been given much, much will be demanded; and from the one who has been entrusted with much, much more will be asked."

We have been entrusted with much, and much more

will be asked of us. Sure, we could say no and go running after things that don't matter, but it's much more fun to step up to the plate when God asks.

I am a fan of superhero movies. In my humble opinion, Batman is the coolest because he does everything he needs to do without any special, superhuman powers. Don't get me wrong—I wouldn't turn down having a superpower; flight or super strength would probably come in handy at some point. Anyway, one theme that comes up over and over in these superhero movies is the theme of responsibility. For instance, when Spider-Man isn't sure what to do with the freaky powers he's

> We have been entrusted with much, and much more will be asked of us.

been given, his uncle Ben pretty much quotes the Bible to him: "With great power comes great responsibility."[3] Then Spider-Man wakes up and realizes he'd better get his grandmother to whip up a suit—because there are a lot of people who need saving.

Same with Batman. He's got every resource money can buy, plus extra-special martial arts training, plus a heart aching for justice. In the movie *Batman Begins*, Bruce Wayne's moment of truth comes when he returns to his home after years of wandering and convinces his butler, Alfred, that he's turned his life around and is committed to fighting injustice. The thing that makes these movies so great is the sharp contrast between good and evil. In *The Dark Knight*, Batman goes above and beyond doing what is right. One of my favorite parts of this movie is the end. After Harvey Dent has enacted his vengeance on the many people he believed wronged him, Batman decides to take the blame.[4] He does what is right even when it's not popular. He uses his responsibility to make a difference. He uses what he has.

The same could be said of you—but it's even cooler because your powers are real, your gifts are in place right now, and God is behind you all the way. When you commit to accepting the responsibility that comes with great power, hold on to your hat—because you're about to change the world for God, and it's going to be better than any comic book or movie you could imagine.

So, to recap, let's think about what we *choose* to focus on. When we focus on what we *don't* have, our hearts are always seeking after that one more thing. They're constantly dissatisfied. But that one thing is never enough, is it? Once you get it, a new craving pops up and you start chasing the next "if only" thing. The things of this world were never meant to satisfy. Jesus says, "What good is it for someone to gain the whole world, and yet lose or forfeit their very self?" (Luke 9:25). What good is it for someone to run after Twinkies and neglect the lunch God made personally? When we choose to focus on what we *do* have—when we're satisfied with the "much" we have been given—God leads us on to the next step. He asks us to live to give, and that's an adventure far greater than chasing after what the world offers.

So the next time we find ourselves pining for something we don't have, thinking that "if only I had this or that, everything would be awesome," let's pray that God will make us content with what we have, that He will make us conscious of and responsible for our gifts and powers, and that He'll show us what new and amazing things He wants us to do with them.

CHOOSING THE TRUTH

The second lesson we can learn from the story of the fall is that we have a few options when it comes to our spiritual gifts. Some of us know exactly what these gifts are and how to continue to foster them. But for others of us, it isn't as easy. Eve had a choice to make between the fruit that God had given her and the fruit that was off limits. It doesn't say it in the Bible, but I am sure she had chosen the other fruit in the garden many times before she chose to eat from the tree. She probably ate breakfast, lunch, and dinner from those good trees every single day. But, eventually, she bought into the lie the serpent so craftily presented in Genesis 3:4-5:

"You will not certainly die," the serpent said to the woman. "For God knows that when you eat of it your eyes will be opened, and you will be like God, knowing good and evil."

Wow! Sounds like a good offer. To be like God? To know good and evil? Maybe if she had a better grasp of what was good and evil, she would have realized that the serpent talking to her was evil.

Have you ever bought into something that sounds like a good offer? What about an infomercial? I wish I hadn't, and I hate to say it, but I have.

"Only $29.95," the man on the TV said. But what he cleverly left out was the other $20 I would spend on shipping and handling. I bought into the tricky lie of getting a "device" that would give me the best abs ever. Rock-hard abs! I have always wanted "six-pack abs." Call me naive or just a guy, but I thought this was the way I was going to get them. Against my dad's wise counsel, I bought it. I thought I would use it a couple of times and then—boom! Out would pop my steel-plated abs.

This device arrived at my door about two weeks later, and when I opened that box up, I was quite surprised. I pulled this "miracle" device out and inserted the pieces. It was made of plastic and some fancy rubber bands. I used the thing a few times, and guess what? I don't have a six pack. I also don't have steel-plated abs. I am not out of shape by any means, but I don't have the thing I was promised. I bought into something I took as the truth when it was actually a lie.

I am not comparing my own stupidity to the fall of mankind, but I do sympathize with the look of surprise Eve must have had when she found out that she wasn't all of a sudden like God. I bought into the lie that this silly ab thing would help me out and make me more like the person I wanted to be. I bought into a lie—a lot like the lies of the world.

The lies of the world can come in many forms, including dissatisfaction and false promises. When it comes to our spiritual gifts, we like to imagine that they will look a certain way. As I said in the last chapter, I really wanted mine to look like me being an amazing basketball player, slam-dunking and ruling the court. Sometimes we think that if God would gift us in the way we want, we could serve Him better. But as we talked about before, that isn't the case. We have to be happy with what God has given us and use that to honor Him.

CHOOSING TO USE YOUR ABILITIES

I recently heard an interesting story about the gazelle. A gazelle is a fast, deer-like creature. Some gazelles can actually reach speeds of up to sixty miles per hour. I have seen numerous gazelles in Africa, and the most interesting thing about gazelles is how high they can jump. A gazelle uses its back legs to spring more than nine feet into the air! Get it a basketball, and it could pretty much dunk. Although these gazelles can jump over nine feet, the walls of their zoo enclosures are typically only three feet tall. Why only three feet? Because if it is raised in captivity, the gazelle doesn't know that it can jump over the fence. A gazelle can clear the fence threefold, but it has never tried.

The moral of the story is that you can't do something if you never try. And you definitely can't do something if you assume, "I can't do that!" You might think you are not good enough, that you can't use what God has given you to make a difference for Him.

Don't believe it. Please know that you *are* good enough, but you might not fully know that until you try. You have gifts capable of changing the world for God, and our enemy is interested in getting you to not even let that lunch box leave the house. Don't buy into that lie.

It's a lie that we shouldn't do anything with what God has given us. Remember that verse about Satan, who goes around like a roaring lion looking for something to devour? If he can't devour your lunch, he will try other ways to make it ineffective. Sometimes we think that it is too late to use a spiritual gift or that we just shouldn't. Sometimes we're afraid it will be too much work. Someone might even have told us that our gift is not worth giving. We think we don't have enough to offer. We don't have enough to make an impact. Not true.

The truth is that we have many ways in which we can nourish what God has given us. If we hide our spiritual gifts and don't do anything with them, we are no better than the servant who does nothing with the talents that his master has given him in Jesus' parable of the talents. Check out this parable in Matthew 25:14–30. Basically, Jesus tells a story about a boss and his three servants. The boss is about to go on a long trip, so he entrusts each servant with a different amount of money to take care of. They called their money *talents*, a lot like we call our money *dollars* in America. Pretty convenient, I think, since we use the talents as a symbol for . . . well . . . talents—and spiritual gifts.

So the man with the most money goes out and puts that money to work, investing it and making a big profit: he doubles his money. When the boss gets back, he's pleased: "Well done, good and faithful servant! You have been faithful with a few things; I will put you in charge of many things. Come and share your master's happiness!" (v. 21). Sounds like an excellent deal, right? Do a little work with what he gives you and then get a giant promotion and get to share happiness with the boss you love? I don't know about you, but these words are the ones I want to hear from God when I tell Him what I've done with my talents.

The fellow with slightly less money has gone out and doubled his money too, and the boss gives him a similar pat on the back. Even though he had about half as much money to start with as the first guy, he didn't feel sorry for himself. He didn't look over at the big profit of his fellow servant and feel so sad or insecure or jealous that he just gave up. No, he did what he could, and got the exact same reaction from the boss when he returned. Another good and faithful servant with an awesome promotion and a share in the boss's happiness.

Then we get to the third guy, who only got one talent to take care of. He says, "I was afraid and went out and hid your gold in the ground. See, here is what belongs to you" (Matthew 25:25). The servant here was afraid of disappointing his master, maybe afraid of losing the gold or looking silly when he tried to invest it. Regardless, he got the opposite reaction from the boss: he got the boot. Why? Because he didn't do anything with what he was given.

Maybe you're afraid of one of the things we talked about above, maybe you're facing one of the lies of this world, or maybe you're just plain discouraged (or afraid of the boot). Don't be! Who knows—you may find out that you're like the gazelle, and you can do many times more than you thought you could. All you had to do was give it a go! Trust in God to make it happen. If God has given us something special inside our lunch boxes, He delights when we use it to serve Him. And like the good and faithful servants, we get to share in His happiness!

STUDY QUESTIONS

1. Have you ever asked God to reveal your gifts to you? If so, what did He show you? If not, see what He does when you ask!

2. What does the idea of a superhero mean to you and how does it affect your outlook on doing good? How can you be a superhero?

3. In the parable of the talents, which servant are you? Who do you want to be?

4. Was there a time in your life when you bought into a lie or a swindle, like the one advertising rock-hard abs? What happened? How can you avoid that in the future?

5. Is there any one particular thing about which you find yourself saying, "Man, if I just had that, everything would be awesome"? Try to notice your impulses and desires this upcoming week, and bring them to God as they pop up.

Grab Your Lunch
and Hit the Road

It was our second trip over to Zambia. We had raised $150,000 to build a medical clinic in the region known as Sinazongwe. The trip was a little bit of a guys' trip. There were eight of us—four adults and four younger guys: my dad's friends (and mine too) Mike Priest and Matt Johnson, as well as some of my friends, Logan Fougnies and Caston Roberts, and their dads, Doug Fougnies and Dan Roberts.

One day we took a trip to see the dedication of the clinic. This place was the first HIV/AIDS testing facility we had built in that region. It provides a way for people who have AIDS to receive testing and treatment for the disease. While there is no drug to cure AIDS, the testing facility finds ways to prolong the lives of those who have the disease. The clinic itself was at the center of a village on the side of a huge, man-made lake full of bugs and all kinds of big spiders—some of which would leap off the wall at us at night! All that to say, it was a little remote. Normally this area has pretty good dirt roads, but we showed up in the middle of the rainy season.

When you visit Africa, one of the first things you notice is the roads. They're not like roads in America, where we have wide, four-lane highways and side streets with traffic lights. In Zambia in particular, the roads are more of the dirt-based variety—not exactly the best for driving. I'm talking four-wheel drive or you're not getting anywhere, especially if you're traveling outside a fairly populated area. Our transportation to this region was not, however, an all-wheel-drive vehicle. It was a big bus. As nice as it was to ride in style (think of a long VW van), the big bus wasn't exactly built for the rainy season in Zambia—and unfortunately for us, that's what was going on. The rain kept pelting down on our bus windows and washing over the loose ground, and pretty soon the road went from dirt to mud. You should know . . .

Big Bus + Mud = a great story for later

The trip down this muddy road was not easy, to say the least. It was normally about a two-hour trip, but it turned into three. All eight of us in the bus clung to the rail above our heads, hanging on for dear life as the bumpy, muddy path continued to get worse. The view from the bus windows wasn't very encouraging either; as we drove along, we saw many trucks pulled off to the side, a little too discouraged to risk being sucked into a giant mud puddle. One was actually flipped on its side! We were nervous that our big bus would suffer the same fate.

The rain was still coming down in sheets about twenty miles outside of Sinazongwe when we came to an abrupt stop. A truck had come toward us, and our driver politely hugged our side of the road a bit too much to let him by. Sure enough, the ground began to shift and the back wheels started to slide to the side of the road. We started to feel a slippery, sickening, tilting feeling, and before we knew it, we hit an embankment. Our bus was now tilting almost sideways in a seven-foot muddy ditch!

We all frantically scrambled to the other side of the bus, trying to even out the weight and keep the bus from flipping. When it became clear that we were firmly lodged in the muck, one by one, we made our way carefully off the bus into the rain. There was no tow company. We were in a pickle. But that's just when things started to get a whole lot brighter.

Meeting people in Africa always changes you, and this moment wasn't any different. Some kids happened by, and they rushed over to help us off the bus. It was like they came out of nowhere! The place was surrounded by trees, but there must have been villages around. Before we knew it, there were about fifteen boys behind the bus, pushing and shouting and trying their hardest to lift the big monster out of the mud. They became absolutely caked in the stuff as the tires spun and mud flew everywhere. But that didn't put a damper on their spirits!

Soon, many more boys showed up and began helping with every ounce of strength they had (and trust me, they had a lot more than I do!). They too got a face full of mud, but within a few minutes the bus's wheels spun free of the grasp of the muddy ditch (with the help of a tractor that came from a nearby village). We stood in the rain and laughed and talked with the boys for a few minutes, grateful for their help and cheered by their smiling faces. We gave them some candy, shook a few hands, and told them all thank you before piling back on the bus and heading on our way.

The rain and the scary situation could have chilled us to the bone, but we were warm inside from these kids' contagious joy. How amazing was it that a bunch of boys who didn't know us wouldn't mind getting dirty to help out? They were traveling along the same scary road we were, but they were willing to give spontaneously to help us through our setbacks (if you can call a giant, sideways, muddy bus in a rainstorm a "setback"). You could say that they shared their lunch with us—on the fly.

●●●●◗●●●●

We can learn a lot from these kids and from this road, because sooner or later, we're all going to head down rough roads of our own. Not literally (well, maybe if you're into off-roading), but figuratively, we're each on a road with Jesus. The journey starts when you give your heart to Him and pledge to use all the gifts in your lunch box for His glory. The goal of the journey is to get to a point where we hand over that lunch to Him and see Him do marvelous things! Then, of course, He sends us out on a new journey, but between point A and point B, we are bound to have some setbacks, maybe even some mudslides, along with some helpful, smiling faces. This chapter is all about hitting the road with your lunch. We're going to talk about how to prepare for the road and about some of the stuff you'll encounter as you begin to take your gifts to Jesus. But before we begin, let's take a little journey back in time.

ONE ANCIENT ROAD TRIP

Imagine with me another road trip that was probably just as tough and bumpy, though probably a lot drier, than our bus adventure in the rainy season. Think about the dust clouds that must have risen off the feet of more than five thousand people as they walked to a remote area near the Sea of Galilee. You guessed it—we're talking about our friend again, the boy with the loaves and fish. This kid's road trip is about as different from our bus trip as you can get, except that it was probably also full of lumps and bumps, potential problems and setbacks.

Do you think the boy had to walk along a road to see Jesus? I think he did. There weren't a lot of transportation options back then aside from carts and animals, but our friend most likely took his own two feet. Now, I'm no expert on the landscape surrounding the Sea of Galilee, but like any outdoor environment, it must have had its uncertainties and dangers. If it is anything like where I grew up in Arizona, I can tell you it may have been full of snakes, scorpions, and lots of sun. Blistering heat, pushy crowds, an uncertain destination, and no Taco Bell drive-through "open till midnight or later." It would have been hard for me to keep going.

Yes, the boy had bundled up his lunch and started

out on a road that may have looked intimidating. But at the end of it—the main attraction: Jesus. This was the man who had been traveling the area, doing miracles, healing the sick, and generally rocking the world of everyone He came in contact with. These people were desperate to get close to Him. Our boy was most likely swept up in the enthusiasm. He had no idea that he and his lunch were about to participate in one of the greatest miracles in the Bible, but he hit the road anyway. And what a long road it was.

The Bible mentions many times that Jesus moved around. John 6:1–2 talks about how Jesus moved through the towns to the other shore of the Sea of Galilee and people followed Him. The account in Mark says that some people actually ran ahead of Him in order to be there as soon as He arrived. I actually measured the map and found that the Sea of Galilee, from shore to shore, is a 19.3-mile walk around the sea. This boy was willing to travel approximately 19.3 miles with his lunch to see Jesus. It could not have been easy at all chugging along for mile after mile, all the time wondering when you can eat a little snack or take a break. But this boy did it. He followed Jesus and let Him use the lunch he had so faithfully carried. The road might not be easy for us either, but let's be ready to carry our lunches all the way. So, are you ready to go?

READY TO SPLIT

Our family recently took an amazing vacation where we got to visit several national parks. While we were at Yellowstone, my dad went to ask a question of a park ranger who was on a bike. The ranger told us, "Just a second." She proceeded to take off her bike helmet and put on her park ranger hat. She then asked my dad what his question was. It was almost as though she had to change hats to answer the question.

A lot of times, though, I find myself thinking like this park ranger. Sometimes I don't give or lend a hand because I am not in the right mode, or even mood. It just isn't the right time. I need to put a different hat on before I can help. But if our friend in John 6 had been thinking like that, he might have missed getting on the road altogether!

It's so easy to think that it just isn't the right time to be used, to think, *Wait! I can't hit this road right now. God can't use me right now.* The truth is, that thinking is false. What if I had thought, *God can't use me right now* when I watched the story of Maggie? What if any of the boys who helped us out of the muddy pit had thought, *I hadn't planned on doing any heavy lifting today, and I really can't stop and get dirty right now?*

Never think that God can't use you in the spur of the moment—that your lunch won't come in handy along the road. God can use you anytime; you just have to be willing. And you have to remember that you are carrying a lunch that is unique and has been packed specially for you. Many times giving your lunch will be a spontaneous act, and sometimes it will happen after you have given a lot of thought to what you are going to do. But there is always a moment of "get-up-and-go" when you decide to start off in the right direc-

> There is always a moment of "get-up-and-go" when you decide to start off in the right direction.

tion. Easier said than done? Yes, but if we can be ready for God to use us, we won't miss the moments while we are changing hats.

FUEL UP

Our Zambian bus driver may not have been an experienced off-roader, but he did a few things right. He filled up that bus with gas. Not only that, but he brought an extra big canister of fuel along in the back of the bus in case we started getting low while we were out in the middle of nowhere. Sure, he hit some muddy problems along the road, but we would have gotten nowhere if we'd run out of gas. The driver had made this long journey before, and he knew enough to make sure the bus's basic needs were covered.

In the same way, we can fuel ourselves for our trip with Jesus, so we have strength to walk along. "How?" you ask. We feed ourselves the good stuff!

Bread: The Word of God

The Bible says, "Man does not live on bread alone but on every word that comes from the mouth of the LORD" (Deuteronomy 8:3). Fortunately for us, God's words went straight from His mouth to the writers of the Bible, and they recorded them there for us to read and study. When we fill up daily on the Word of God, we'll be full of all sorts of things—and a better kind of full than you get from eating a dozen dinner rolls. Filling up on the Word will give us:

- Light in a dark place (2 Peter 1:19; Psalm 119:105)
- Encouragement and hope (Romans 15:4)
- Fearlessness, virtue, and knowledge (Psalm 56:4; 2 Peter 1:5)
- Equipment for every good work (2 Timothy 3:16–17)
- A never-ending supply of love (Romans 8:38–39)

I'll take it! If I'm full of all these things next time I hit a bump or a rough spot in my road, I'll be much better off than I would be without them, don't you think? The Bible is an amazing source of fuel. Spend some time with it every day, and you'll find yourself getting more revved up than you ever thought possible.

"But, Austin," you might say, "have you ever *read* Deuteronomy?" I will tell you the truth: I have tried to get through it. But I will start today to try and finish it if you do too. Let's be honest. If the Bible doesn't seem like the most thrilling thing you can think of to read, you're not the only one who feels that way. Don't give up on it, though. Start small with the Psalms or one of the Gospels, and take advantage of the many good guided Bible studies out there, meant to help you get started.

I used to use the old "Flip-Open-the-Bible-and-Point-and-Wherever-Your-Finger-Lands-That-Is-What-You-Should-Read" method. Also known as the FOTBPWYFLTIWYSR method. I am not saying there is anything wrong with this method, or that there isn't a shorter acronym somewhere, but you can find some more organized, purposeful studies at your local bookstore, for free online, or even on your cell phone, all arranged around a variety of topics.

What's going on in your life right now? Chances are there's a Bible study tailor-made to address your challenges or interests at this very moment. Ask for recommendations from your pastor or some other Bible-loving person you know. Better yet, get involved in a Bible study. There's nothing better than eating with friends, right? In the same way, studying the Bible with others can be like going from eating alone in your room to hitting your favorite local spot with ten other hungry pals. It just makes things go down easier. No matter how you do it, make sure you fuel up with this staple: the Word of God.

Living Water: Prayer and the Spirit

Okay, so I don't typically fill up on too much water before a long car trip. You know. Nobody wants to stop every half hour to answer the call of nature. But if you're walking or hiking in the heat and hauling your lunch along with you, not getting enough water can be a really, really bad thing. Dehydration can cause weakness, dizziness, fainting, and even more serious problems if it goes untreated.[1] Not what you want to happen on the road. Water is essential.

Jesus talks about another kind of water that's just as essential: living water. A story in John tells us that the Lord runs into a woman at a well and asks her for a drink. The woman is shocked that a man like Him would even talk to a Samaritan woman like her—Jews and Samaritans did not associate—and she wonders why He would ask her such a thing. "Jesus answered her, 'If you knew the gift of God and who it is that asks you for a drink, you would have asked him and he would have given you living water'" (4:10). Living water. He's not talking about the kind of water that comes from a stream as opposed to a well ("living" instead of "still"). Instead, He is talking about the kind of water that refreshes our hearts and souls, that "[wells] up to eternal life" (v. 14). That's salvation and the Spirit of God—His Holy Spirit inside of us. And how did He tell the woman she can get this living water? She can ask Him for it.

We ask God for things in prayer. We get close to Him that way. We spend time with Him, get to know Him, learn to enjoy His presence, and listen to what He wants. We grow in our love for Him and our desire to live to give. And once that living water gets flowing, it helps us to keep praying! "The Spirit helps us in our weakness. We do not know what we ought to pray for, but the Spirit himself intercedes for us" (Romans 8:26). This living water is the real deal. It refreshes us (Psalm 104:30), teaches us (Luke 12:12), gives us life (2 Corinthians 3:6), and fills us with power (Micah 3:8). It's something I think we all need every day.

Prayer is how we get there.

If you're not sure how best to pray, check out Matthew 6:9–13 for some detailed instructions. You can also find good prayer resources in books, online, and from your pastors. Prayer, along with reading God's Word, will get us fueled. Every day. Before we head out onto the road or start huffing up dry, dusty hills, we've got to be hydrated. We've got to have something in our stomachs.

We've got to have some fuel! And not just a little bit, but a full tank for those times in the mud.

PACK YOUR BAGS

So if we're fueled up and ready to go at a moment's notice, then what? Get ready to run out the door! Many times, before I leave the house on a long trip, I do a quick spot check. Do I have my keys? My toothbrush? My phone? My wallet? After reaching in my bag a million times and patting all my pockets, I finally feel ready to leave. I can rest a little easier about the journey and pay attention to other things, knowing that I won't show up at my destination and be lost without some item or another.

But on our journeys with Jesus, we only need a few things—and the big one is *your lunch*. Don't leave that thing sitting on the counter, getting mushy and smelly while you run off without it. Your gifts and talents are in there, and God wants to use them!

Imagine if David just so happened to have forgotten his slingshot the day he went out to meet Goliath. That would have been a bummer. What if the boy in John 6 had forgotten his lunch that day? Could you imagine? I'm sure Jesus could have just used rocks or something else cool, but it would have made the story a lot different, and one less boy would have gotten to help be a part of a miracle.

So how do we forget our lunches? Don't we often forget to bring along the gifts, the talents, the tools that God gave us to help change the world? The answer for me is yes. Many times I find myself wishing I had decided to help out in an instance or make a difference in a certain place. But I didn't. When I look back at these times, I feel a little regret. It wouldn't have taken much to really bless someone, but instead all I have is a missed opportunity. Depressing, huh? Think back to the last time you really wished you'd spoken up for someone or given to someone, or used your lunch in some other way. It's not a good feeling, is it? Even worse than opening up your duffel bag and discovering you have no underwear for the next week.

If our boy in John 6 had forgotten his lunch that day, he might have been left standing in the crowd, just wishing he had remembered his lunch so he could offer it to Jesus when it was needed. Fortunately, he didn't forget it—and Jesus used it to bless many people and give us an unforgettable story. Take a minute and recall the gifts you discovered in the last chapter. Write them down, reflect on them, and say a quick prayer of thanks to God that He put those gifts in your lunch box. Keep a firm grip on them, and you'll remember them when the time comes!

Take a look at some of the gifts God may have given you. Create the ones that you think may fit you.

Public speaking

Writing

Self-management

Networking (person to person)

Networking (virtual world)

Critical thinking

Decision making

Math

History

English

Science

Relaxation

Accounting

Bookkeeping

The law

Marketing

Advertising

Graphics

Art

Drawing

Photography

Woodworking

Creating videos

Developing websites

Programming

Jokes/humor

Creativity

Innovation

Foreign language

Sign language

Teaching/training

Negotiating

Planning

Leadership

Listening

Reading

Persuading

Typing

Taking initiative

Future thinking

Analyzing the past

Inspiring

Storytelling

Communication skills

Project management

Sales

Problem solving

Detail orientation

Social intelligence

Recruiting people

Self-control

Health/fitness

Dexterity

Juggling

Visualization

Adaptability

Imagination

Athleticism

People judgment

Awareness

Integrity/honesty

Empathy

Self discipline

Encouraging

Software development

Computers/IT

Managing money

Dealing with adults

Brainstorming

Making connections

Ability to handle change

Conflict resolution

Maintenance/routine tasks

Futuristic

Fairness

Crafts

Painting

Social networking (online)

Listening to people

Giving hugs

Comforting people

Fixing things

Planting and growing things

Enjoying nature

Flower arranging

Yard work

Working on cars or machines

Getting your point across

Organizing

Collecting

Coaching

Taking care of animals

Cheering people up

Serving people

Charity work

Having new ideas

Sculpting

Researching

Imagining

Making up stories

Problem solving

Cooking

Eating!

Making observations

Acting

Singing

Knitting

Playing a musical instrument

Being a mega-fan

Fashion

Design

Weight lifting

Exploring

Having compassion

The truth is that all of us have amazing spiritual gifts. That list is the very tip of the iceberg. God has given you a plethora of gifts—not just one. Start embracing them today!

STUDY QUESTIONS

1. WHAT IS THE ROAD LIKE IN YOUR LIFE RIGHT NOW? SMOOTH? BUMPY? WHY?
2. HOW CAN BEING PREPARED HELP YOU IN BUMPY MOMENTS?
3. HOW CAN YOU "FUEL UP" IN YOUR DAILY LIFE? MAKE A LIST OF SPECIFIC WAYS YOU CAN RECHARGE AND PREPARE WITH BOTH SPIRITUAL BREAD AND WATER.
4. ARE YOU SURPRISED BY ANY OF THE THINGS YOU CIRCLED ON THE LIST OF POSSIBLE GIFTS? WHAT GIFTS WOULD YOU ADD TO THE LIST? WHAT'S THE THING YOU THOUGHT LEAST LIKELY TO BE A TRUE SPIRITUAL GIFT?
5. HOW CAN YOU BE READY TO GET UP AND GO IF YOU'RE SUDDENLY CALLED ON TO USE YOUR GIFT?

When It Gets Bumpy

You're out the door! You've got your lunch! You're following Jesus, getting ready to discover how He wants to use your gifts. That's amazing! You're about to see some incredible things come to pass. When you finally do get to give your lunch away, what a feeling it is! But because you're on the road, and the road can be a tough place, it pays to be prepared. You're fueled up on prayer and the Word of God. Now get ready for the mud. You may get spattered, splashed, and knocked about, but if you know what to expect, you can brace yourself. Here are a few things that might keep you from using the gifts in your lunch box.

WHAT-IFS

Starting out on a long trip can be exciting—and a little nerve-racking too. Have you ever been hit with an attack of the pre-travel jitters? You get nervous and start asking yourself all sorts of paranoid questions: *What if I make a wrong turn? What if I forget my toothbrush? What if I get lost or lose my parents? Or if the place we're going doesn't have a snack machine? What if my bus falls sideways in a ditch? What if?* Have you ever asked those what-if questions? All those what-ifs can get you so flustered that they might make it hard to begin down the road to giving your lunch to Jesus. You might think, *What if I go for this and it doesn't work? Won't I look stupid? What if this turns out to be really, really hard?*

I'm going to be honest with you. The road with Jesus is not all sunshine and smooth sailing. Things do go wrong. Things do get tough. Sometimes you do end up without a toothbrush or sideways in a ditch. Jesus tells us, "In this world you will have trouble." Note the word *will*. We will have trouble. Great, huh? (I can see you reaching for that paper bag to breathe into.) "But," He adds, "but take heart! I have overcome the world" (John 16:33). Jesus has control of your situation. He doesn't need your help, remember, but He does want it. He is able to work all things for the good of those who love Him—even wrong turns, lack of snack machines, or harder, more serious mishaps (Romans 8:28). He has more good advice: "Can any one of you by worrying add a single hour to your life?" (Matthew 6:27). In fact, worry only takes away hours of your life. It takes away from your lunch. When you get hit with a fit of what-ifs on the road, combat them with the truth of Jesus' words and keep your eyes on Him!

CROWDED STREETS

The boy in John 6 was part of "a great crowd of people" (v. 2) who followed Jesus to hear what He had to say. What would it be like to be in the midst of a "great crowd"? Probably lively, colorful, and loud. Today, our lives are just as crowded. It doesn't matter how young or old you are—there's always something vying for your attention. TV, movies, video games, iPods, iPhones, work, sports, clubs, family, hobbies, school, travel, friends—the list goes on and on.

One of the places I have experienced a big crowd of people is the airport. I've been in some pretty big ones, but the "Great Wall of China" of airports is in London, England. Sure, airports in America can become chaotic, to say the least, but London's trumps them all for me. Every time I fly through there I am met by the massive crowd of people all standing in line to get rescreened through security. Nobody is in a particularly good mood, considering the lines can take close to an hour. Chaos? Yes. Security personnel are shouting about open lines, buzzers are going off every second, not to mention the auditorium feel, which adds reverb to all the noise. This "great crowd" made the "road" to my airplane a little different.

But if the boy was in this "great crowd," I am sure that the road to Jesus wasn't easy either. Could you imagine following this dirt path for miles just to see Jesus? I'm sure there were plenty of opportunities to take detours or get caught up in the hype of the situation. It says in John 6:2 that the "great crowd" followed Jesus because He did signs and miracles, which is amazing, of course. But will we follow Him because He is the Savior of the world? Because He is good, and what He does is good (Psalm 119:68)? It is a hard question but a worthwhile one. Will you go the 19.3 miles for God alone? If you find yourself getting distracted, don't beat yourself up. Just gently redirect your attention and take a minute to pray for guidance as you keep on walking that road.

ROAD NARROWS

Think back to my African bus story and imagine yourself as the bus. Imagine you're bumping down a muddy, unpaved path on your journey with Jesus, with rain lashing your windows. Can you imagine feeling a little lost, a little scared, a little hesitant? Sometimes we think that we don't belong on this road, that maybe it would be better if we took a safer route. But God knows the path we should be on, and there are rewards for those who walk the difficult road.

Have you ever run into one of these signs while driving?

It means that the four-lane road you're on may be going down to two lanes soon, or that the nice wide lanes in the flatlands are about to change to a precarious goat trail in the mountains. Those always remind me of a verse in Matthew 7, which says:

> Enter through the narrow gate. For wide is the gate and broad is the road that leads to destruction, and many enter through it. But small is the gate and

narrow the road that leads to life, and only a few find it. (vv. 13–14)

That verse is like a Road Narrows sign. It tells us that God rewards those who go on the narrow, muddy road. The road may be difficult, but it is worth it. Remember our conversation about the temptations and distractions of this world? Those temptations point us down a wide, paved, easy road, promising fulfillment in things like money, power, fame, success, popularity, and "stuff." That road may seem sweet and easy, but it's taking you nowhere fast—"to destruction." If you're trudging along, slipping and sliding all over the place, and you look over and see people whizzing by on the wide road, don't get discouraged. Stick with the narrow road, however muddy it may be, because obeying God always pays off with "life"—and life "abundantly" (John 10:10 KJV)!

We have already mentioned this, but the common misconception is that serving God is easy. Many times it is not. Never let that discourage you from going down that road, but do realize it can be tough. Challenges can and probably will occur, and many of those will simply be from the uncertainty that you face. You may wonder, *Will this really work? Does God really want me to use my gift? Am I going to get stuck out here in the middle of nowhere?* God does want you to be on this road, and through Him you can do it. We will talk more about these doubts later, but for now, remember that God would not call you to the road if you could not make it. Remember Philippians 1:6: "The God who started this great work in you [will] keep at it and bring it to a flourishing finish on the very day Christ Jesus appears" (MSG).

> God would not call you to the road if you could not make it.

ROAD CREW

Once, I was guarding another person during a soccer game on a wet field. I was a little uncertain, as he was faster than I was. As determined as I was not to fall, I ended up slipping in one of the mud pools along the soccer field. My teammates, though, were right there to cheer me on and encourage me to chase the kid down. Plus, mud kinda looks cool on a soccer uniform. You look really tough. Like Bear Grylls, *Man vs. Wild* status.

The road toward giving your lunch isn't easy, but it sure can become a lot easier if you let those around you encourage you and push you a little. You might think that you don't have anybody, but you do!

Think back to the boys who helped our bus on the side of the road. These boys are my favorite part of the story. They were so selfless and so willing to serve. They weren't worried about getting mud on themselves as long as it meant they could help us out. These boys represent those people around you who are standing on the side of the road cheering you on, ready to push you out of a ditch if you need it. Your road crew might be made up of family, friends, church members, pastors, mentors, or any other group of loving, God-following supporters. Sometimes they're even complete strangers, like the boys in Africa.

Sometimes you come to a ditch that seems too hard to handle. But you don't have to go through it alone. God gifts us with people who are willing to get mud all over themselves if it means that we will be able to be on our way sooner. I couldn't have started Hoops of Hope in a million years if it weren't for the overwhelming support of my sister, my parents, my grandparents, and my friends. It seemed as if everyone was cheering for me, and when I slipped in the mud of uncertainty, they were there to pull me out.

You have people around you who want to encourage and help you out of the mud. What about your youth pastor? Try starting there. If you're not sure where your road crew is, pray about it. Ask God to bring people to mind or into your life who can be on your road crew—and people who can use you on theirs. Remember,

Two are better than one, because they have a good return for their labor: If either of them falls down, one can help the other up. But pity anyone who falls and has no one to help them up. Also, if two lie down together, they will keep warm. But how can one keep warm alone? Though one may be overpowered, two can defend themselves. A cord of three strands is not quickly broken. (Ecclesiastes 4:9–12)

Whether it's a road crew of one, two, ten, or a hundred, help from others is critical. Let them help you out of the mud.

SANDAL SHOCK

People in the Bible went through a lot of sandals. I am actually going to venture to say that mostly everyone wore sandals. I have nothing to back that up, of course, other than the mention of sandals in the Bible itself. Can you imagine having to follow Jesus around in sandals? I mean, it takes a pretty dedicated person to follow Jesus as much as He moved while teaching, but in sandals? I would want a nice pair of comfortable sneakers to walk in, but as we Christians know the road of following Jesus isn't always comfortable—just as the road to giving your lunch to Jesus isn't either.

Sometimes it is a muddy or dusty road that you have to wear sandals on. It can be filled with rocks, what-ifs, crowds, and narrow passageways. But if we leave our what-ifs on the side of the road, fuel up, and ask for help from our friends, it will make the road a lot easier. We don't have to go down the road alone; we have God right there with us. So stay on that road, walking joyfully toward Jesus.

STUDY QUESTIONS

1. WHAT HAS BEEN THE MOST RECENT ROADBLOCK IN YOUR JOURNEY THROUGH LIFE? HOW ABOUT IN YOUR SPIRITUAL LIFE?

2. HOW DO YOU DEAL WITH MUD OR ROADBLOCKS WHEN THEY STAND IN YOUR WAY?

3. DO YOU HAVE A "ROAD CREW"? WHO ARE THEY? IF NOT, HOW WILL YOU GO ABOUT FINDING ONE?

4. THE ROAD TO JESUS WASN'T AN EASY ONE BY ANY MEANS. ARE YOU READY TO GO THE 19.3 MILES? THINK OF A FEW WAYS YOU CAN GET READY TO DO THIS TODAY.

8

Your Biggest Fear: Fear

It seems like it takes forever to get to Africa. From the times I've been, I can tell you that it is a long, hard trip. Besides the nine-hour time difference, the journey itself is pretty epic. It starts from my home in Phoenix, Arizona, with a flight to Detroit. Detroit takes us to London, and from London we fly into Lusaka, Zambia—the capital. All in all, at times it has taken a grand total of forty hours to go one way with layovers. After we land, we have another two days of driving before we make it to the southern part of Zambia where Hoops of Hope has done a lot of work.

Have you ever been on a journey like that? A long journey that seems as though it would never end? With all the flights and driving, I thought it might not ever end the first time I did it. I can tell you that once I got there, though, it was so worth it. I would do it time and time again because of how great the payoff is. Most of the time, the hardest trips have the best rewards at the end.

Picture this. You're part of a huge herd of people, shuffling quickly along a dusty road. You're following Jesus around the edge of a massive lake with at least five thousand people you might not know. You can see Jesus, a dot in the distance, but He is pretty far ahead. You're just a young kid being swept along with the crowd. There are many people around you, yet, somehow, you feel alone. Maybe it would have been a little bit easier if someone from your family had come along with you, you think. You don't really know what you're doing—all you know is that you have to hear what the teacher has to say; you'd grabbed your lunch and headed out after Him that morning.

The 19.3 miles seem to stretch out before you, farther and farther. You start to wonder if the great teacher, Jesus, will ever stop to take a break and teach. As you continue to walk, your stomach starts to rumble. Your feet start to ache from those sandals. Step after step, you grasp your small lunch tighter in your palms, squishing it a bit. *Maybe I should stop and take a few bites just to keep me going*, you start to think. That's when it hits you. You look from side to side to see if anyone is snacking, but no one is. Then you realize you are the only one carrying a lunch. *Awkward!*

Has everyone forgotten their lunches? You look at the food in your hands and begin to feel a little self-conscious. *Am I the weird kid for actually having a lunch? Maybe I should leave it right here and grab it on the way home* . . . Then you see some of the bigger boys start to elbow each other and point at what you're carrying. Those snickers can mean only one thing: they're making fun of your lunch. One of them starts teasing you about the fishy smell coming out of the packet, and another one asks if your mom writes you love notes and puts them in your lunch every day. They high-five each other. All of a sudden, the 19.3 miles just got a whole lot lonelier. To make matters worse, on top of being a bit bored, hungry, and thirsty, now you feel *different*.

THE SCARIEST THING

I conducted a short poll for this book, asking people to choose what scared them the most off of a list of typically frightening things.[1] The number one answer wasn't snakes, dying, public speaking, spiders, heights, water, the dark, terrorism, clowns, or the divorce of parents. The scariest thing was "not being accepted." A total of 59.8 percent of participants were afraid of it. That blows me away! I would never guess when faced with things that are intentionally supposed to strike fear into us, like terrorism and clowns, not being accepted was viewed as the worst. I have to be honest with you, though: it is one of my biggest fears as well. Along with "not being accepted," other top choices in the poll included "being made fun of" (40.2 percent), tied in second place with "being alone" (40.2 percent). I think we all sympathize.

Off of this list, please select each that is a fear of yours.

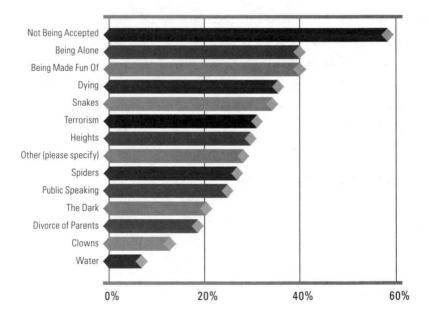

Here's a hard fact of life: when it comes to making a difference in this world, when it comes to having an impact, you will experience a lot of these fearsome things. *But* if we can properly learn how to deal with them as they arise, we can keep them from sucking away our spirit and getting us stuck in the mud. How? Well, for each of these hurtful things, God has provided an uplifting antidote.

NOT ACCEPTED

Not being accepted causes a terrible, sinking sensation that happens to people across generational and gender gaps. It happens to all of us at times in our lives—and usually not just once. You know. It's when you walk into a room and people whom you thought liked you start giving you the cold shoulder. It can even come from strangers, who for some reason decide you're not like them or up to their standards. Ouch! When you go to make a difference, when you set out to use the gifts in your lunch box, you have to realize that you may not be accepted. As the Bible verse said earlier, the road we are called to follow is straight and narrow (Matthew 7:14). Few find it, and therefore those who haven't found it are oftentimes not accepting of those who have. Why is this?

To be honest with you, I don't have the answer to this one. Sometimes, when we're following God, those close to us aren't accepting of what we are doing. I don't have the answer to exactly why, but I can tell you that I've experienced this firsthand.

It will happen to you. It might look a little different when it does, but it happens to all of us. All of us will go past this on the road. Some will give up and just become roadkill, but you can stick it out to the end. How do we stick it out? We have to remain focused on what truly matters: God and the people we are helping!

But what's the antidote to not being accepted? It's realizing who your real friends are. Your real friends begin to come out when you stop being accepted. They give you fist bumps and walk beside you when others are giving you icy glares or making fun of you. There were a few true friends who came out in support of me. Those friends encouraged me to continue down the road. They built me up when I was in a tough place. You will find that you might be hardly accepted at all, but God will put a few people along the road with you to help you. They're one of His greatest gifts.

Yes, there are those who might say that you should be able to shrug it off and not care about acceptance. "Sticks and stones may break my bones, but words can never hurt me." I can tell you that this doesn't work. No matter how much I told myself acceptance didn't matter, it still did in the back of my mind. If you can stick with your true friends, be thankful for them, focus on your mission, and get to a state where you couldn't care less about acceptance, that is a good thing. If you can look for acceptance from God and from your support system, you will be able to continue down the road. After all, God gave one of the most rejected people of all time, His Son, a group of twelve men to walk with Him on His way. God won't leave you stranded on the side of the road.

BEING MADE FUN OF

The next big fear in my informal poll was "being made fun of." And we're not talking about joking, like "Your mama's so stupid she thinks Taco Bell is a Mexican phone company." If you're made fun of on a regular basis, it can be very draining. It's something we don't really want to have to go through, but it does happen at times. Most people are generally pretty well mannered, of course, but sometimes meanness wins out. I have had it happen to me before too. It can come in the form of a harmless joke that hits a little too close to home, and other times it can come from some really intensely offended person lashing out like a springing viper, stinging you with an insult. But let me remind you of what Matthew 5:10 says: "Blessed are those who are persecuted because of righteousness, for theirs is the kingdom of heaven."

Being made fun of might hurt for a moment, but it's like burning your finger on a hot pan. It's annoying and maybe painful while it stings, but it goes away. But if it goes beyond that—if you are persecuted for the name of Jesus—the Bible says *blessed* are you (Matthew 5:10). Sure, that sounds like a blessing you'd rather not get, but God knows exactly how much we can take. Those who are persecuted for His name are blessed.

The antidote for being made fun of is remembering you're blessed and thanking God for it. So my encouragement to you on this topic is to do something a little different the next time someone hurls an insult. Instead of sniping back or feeling terrible about yourself, say to yourself, "I am blessed." Because you are. Think of Paul, who went through some pretty terrible stuff for doing God's work. He said,

Who shall separate us from the love of Christ? Shall trouble or hardship or persecution or famine or nakedness or danger or sword? As it is written:

"For your sake we face death all day long;
we are considered as sheep to be
slaughtered."

No, in all these things we are more than conquerors through him who loved us. For I am convinced that neither death nor life, neither angels nor demons, neither the present nor the future, nor any powers, neither height nor depth, nor anything else

in all creation, will be able to separate us from the
love of God that is in Christ Jesus our Lord. (Romans
8:35–39 NIV 1984)

BEING ALONE

The next most common thing people were scared of in
my survey was "being alone." It's a tough thing to deal
with for anybody. We want to follow Jesus 19.3 miles like
our boy did, but there is a possibility that we will have
to do it alone at times. That thought is very scary. God
knows that we were not meant to be alone. I think that's
why He has such sympathy for people who are left all on
their own in the world—orphans and widows. In fact, the
book of James says, "Religion that God our Father accepts
as pure and faultless is this: to look after orphans and
widows in their distress and to keep oneself from being
polluted by the world" (1:27 NIV 1984).

Right now in Africa, more than 15 million children
have been orphaned because of AIDS. The charitable organization Orphan's Hope estimates 143 million children
are orphaned in the world right now.[2] It is such a big
number that it is hard for us to wrap our minds around it.
But if 143 million orphaned children were to link hands
and stand in a single line, they would wrap around the
world three times. Loneliness is around us, but it should
not paralyze us. Just as God is with the widow and the

orphan, He is with us when we are lonely. As He reaches out to us, we can reach out to others, like these orphans.

Do you think the boy with the loaves and fish walked alone before the time came for him to share his gift? The Bible doesn't tell us specifically, but imagine if he had gone by himself to see Jesus, not with his friends or his family. I am sure along the way he would have experienced being made fun of or not being accepted. After all, he was the only kid with a lunch. He was different in that sense. Ultimately, I believe, he probably experienced loneliness at some point.

Out of each of these top fears, loneliness is the most paralyzing. We many times don't want to walk down that road by ourselves. We wish someone were next to us. We don't want to get out there and do something and then find ourselves in the dark. But if we are going to do something bigger than ourselves, our comfort zones will be breached. It is much more comfortable to have all our friends around us and to stay in this tight little circle, but we can't do that.

> If we are going to do something bigger than ourselves, our comfort zones will be breached.

Before you step out into making a difference you will ask yourself, *What if I'm alone? What if nobody supports me? What if nobody cares about what I'm doing? What if my youth pastor doesn't like my idea? What if none of my friends think it's cool?*

Well, I can tell you firsthand that being alone is not fun. My pastor supported me and my family supported me, but many times my friends didn't. On my very first event day, when I was nine, Channel 12 News did an interview with me that night. I remember how excited and tired I was. The newscaster asked me, "So, Austin, you think you'll be pretty popular at school tomorrow?" My response was, "Just for one day!"

Sometimes you might find yourself being the only one making a difference. You might find yourself being the only one who truly cares about a cause. It can be difficult to find the strength to move on. But I can tell you when you step out of your comfort zone, when you do something bigger than yourself, you are never alone. God says in Hebrews 13:5, "Never will I leave you; never will I forsake you." And I believe with all my heart that promise is just as real to you and me today. So when we find ourselves in a spot of loneliness, I can promise you that you are *never* alone. I am truly thankful for that promise.

••••◦••

My friend Justin lives in Philadelphia. Justin is a person who wanted to make a difference in the world with what

God had given him. So Justin decided to raise money and do a Hoops of Hope event. Justin ended up raising a ton of money by shooting hoops all day long.

What if fear had paralyzed Justin? What if he had been scared that people would think he was weird? What if he had gotten bored and lonely after the first hundred hoops and decided to go hang out with his buddies instead? But he didn't. He knew the antidote to fear, which is remembering your purpose.

If everyone wanting to do a Hoops of Hope event were overcome with fear of one of these three things—being unaccepted, made fun of, or alone—they could let it keep them from using what God gave them. A lot of things would be different in the world if that were the case. For starters, Hoops of Hope wouldn't exist, and neither would the projects its funds are used for.

Imagine a new computer lab at the local high school in Zambia. It's in the middle of nowhere. You have to drive on bumpy roads for about four hours from the nearest city, but this school has a computer lab. Inside it are brand-new computers actually built into the back of a shipping container. They are solar powered and easy to maintain out in the boonies, and they provide libraries upon libraries of information for the people using them. Why are these computers so important? Because if you know how to use a computer in Zambia, you have a much better chance of getting into college and getting a job. That's a huge deal. But here's something even more amazing about this lab: it's the only one in the entire country. It isn't in the city; it's in a rural area, providing knowledge to the poorest of people.

Chilala Clinic Solar

What if Hoops of Hope participants had been held back by fear? What if one of the people, who (like me) wasn't very good at basketball, was afraid of being made fun of for missing shots? African students might not be attending college. They might not have the chance to succeed that they now have. If people like Justin had been held back by fear, these students might not go on to be the doctors and teachers they strive to be.

What if the boy in John 6 had been held back by fear? What if he'd decided not to go that day? What if he had left his lunch by the road? If that had happened, five thousand people might have gone hungry that day.

There might be five thousand people needing to be fed by what you have. You have the chance to make an impact. Don't let fear keep you from knowing the joy of feeding others with your lunch. God is not the author of fear, but God will deliver you from it. Know your friends, thank God for your blessings, and keep your eye on the prize of helping others. When you start out on the road after Jesus, keep going step-by-step, and soon those 19.3 miles will be behind you.

STUDY QUESTIONS

1. Have you ever thought a journey would never end? Describe that time. How did you feel when it was finally over? Was there something good at the end?
2. What is your reaction to loneliness on the road? How do you deal with it?
3. What makes being lonely hard for you?
4. What is the thing that keeps you going?
5. What kinds of fears might keep you from starting your 19.3 miles? How can you counteract them?

9

Hungry

Hunger can make us do crazy things. Do you find yourself turning into a different person when you are hungry? I tend to go on a snacking rampage and raid the pantry. Hunger can also turn all of us into food-seeking missiles. You might rummage through your kitchen with laser focus, throwing together a bizarre snack of Fruity Pebbles and eggnog. You may stop at the McDonald's you promised you would never eat at after you saw that documentary on fast food. In the face of the three-o'clock munchies, that squished, half-eaten candy bar collecting dust in the pocket of your backpack starts to look pretty good.

Yes, we all do things we would never do in our right minds just because of simple hunger. We still have it pretty easy, though. In the face of natural disasters or famine, normal, honest people find themselves suddenly willing to steal because of hunger, even if they may never have done that otherwise. Angry, hungry mobs have toppled governments all throughout history, and they still do.

Hunger can drive us in one of two ways: toward good or toward bad. On the good side, we can use our hunger—physical, mental, or spiritual—to fuel us to do better in the world or go to lengths we would never attempt if we were full and comfortable. For example, the farmers in Twachiyanda, Zambia, are some of the hardest-working people I have ever seen. They work fields of dry, unfertile soil year-round to grow corn. Their days start at sunrise and end way past sunset, and they endure backbreaking labor. It takes a lot of genius and ingenuity to get water into that ground and coax plants to come up out of the near-desert, but they do it because hunger is a powerful motivation. Most of these farmers are subsistence farmers; this means they only grow enough to feed their families. Hunger—survival—is the reason they work so hard. It fuels them to work harder than I would have thought humanly possible. In the same way, this kind of focused passion can move us to action.

Think about it. You could be hungry for that baseball

championship; you feel the need to push yourself further and further in practice, stretching your abilities so you can take home the trophy. You can be hungry for good grades, so you keep studying long after you're tired and you want to quit. You can be hungry for fame, money, success, beauty, and all sorts of worldly things. But you can also be hungry for God's will to be done—hungry to do good. When you look at the needs around you (or even within you), your spiritual stomach might start to growl, helping you focus on the God who feeds us in every way imaginable (Psalm 146:7). That's the good kind of hunger!

SOGGY LUNCH VERSUS JESUS-STYLE FEAST

What about the story of the feeding of five thousand? Don't you think hunger played a huge role there? After all, those people had followed Jesus around for 19.3 miles; it was time for a meal, to say the least. This great moving force motivated Andrew to find the boy with the lunch. It moved the people to begin to stand up because they were so hungry (John 6:10). Hunger made the miracle necessary. If they weren't hungry . . . no need for a miracle.

Hunger must have played a big role on the road too. I have often wondered how many people might have been present if it hadn't been necessary to walk all the way to the other side of the Sea of Galilee. Might there have been six thousand people at the beginning? Maybe ten thousand? How many started and turned around?

If stomachs work today the way they did back then, I am sure this was the case. I don't know about you, but even thinking about a 19.3-mile walk makes me hungry—let alone doing it! Picture yourself, having not eaten anything all day, walking around this giant sea to hear Jesus. You realize there is a great fish taco shack right over there off the main road. Do you break off from the group and stop? Do you turn around or keep going? I bet if there had been little Taco Bell carts along that road, they would have made a lot of money that day.

Personally, I am amazed by those thousands of people who made it all the way. They let their need to see Jesus outweigh their physical comfort. I am amazed by them because I don't know if I could have done it if I had been in their shoes. Their faith was strong, but so was the spiritual hunger that drove them to continue.

WORTH THE WAIT

Let's talk some more about my favorite foods. Really—this never gets old for me. This time I want to turn your attention to the marvelous, cheesy, crusty miracle of the creation we call pizza. Like most red-blooded American kids, I love the stuff. A lot of times a little microwave pizza will satisfy the craving and keep me going. Sure, the crust is a bit floppy and wet in the middle and the cheese may taste weird. But it's food of the pizza-flavored variety, so I don't complain. But then . . . *then* there is real, live Chicago-style pizza. The kind in the deep dish, made by a real Chicagoan.

It is a pizza masterpiece: crusty on the outside, chewy on the inside, with bubbly cheese and toppings cooked to perfection. The thing is, it can take forty-five minutes to bake. Forty-five minutes! I could pass out in forty-five minutes! But is it worth the wait? No question about it: *yes.* Putting microwaved up against restaurant-baked, Chicago-style pizza would be like putting a stick figure up against the Sistine Chapel. Like many good things, it's *worth the wait.*

As you may have noticed or will notice, when you begin making a difference, you'll want to see results right away. When we don't see those results, it can be hard for us to want to continue. Many times we might think that what we are doing just doesn't work, or that we are doing it wrong. This might not be the case. Keep following that rumble in your tummy.

If there were people who quit that day by the Sea of Galilee, they missed out on what I consider the most amazing miracle in the Bible. They may have missed out because they let their hunger drive them toward a quick fix rather than a real meal. They may have missed out because they didn't know how much farther it was going to be. Sometimes waiting can be a hard thing to do.

My mom and I grow a garden every year. The first time we did it, we actually built the garden bed out of wood ourselves. We set the frame in the perfect spot and dumped soil into it. Then we filled it full of plants and vegetables just waiting to produce some amazing, fresh, tasty, garden-grown food. Our planters were bursting with tomatoes, many kinds of peppers, squash, strawberries, chives, and parsley. Even though we had bought the plants already partially grown so they would produce quickly, it wasn't until a few months later that we actually started to see some results. Those few months felt like *forever*. During that time we watered the garden daily, plucked out the weeds, built a small fence to keep birds out, and even rescued birds that had gotten caught in that fence. But only after time could we enjoy the fruit of our labor; the world's best salad was even better because of the work we'd put into it.

Isn't making a difference a little like Chicago-style pizza or our garden? Many times we think we can just start with an idea and the next day a school will be built in Africa. I remember that after I was given the idea for Hoops of Hope, I wanted to go shoot my baskets the next day. But I couldn't. I had to wait and water my garden. You see, if I had shot baskets the next day, I wouldn't have had time to get the word out or raise any money.

If I hadn't raised any money, I wouldn't have seen any results. Waiting and watering take time, but they are crucial. Making a difference in the world is a marathon, not a sprint. We sometimes have to realize that all great things take time. The longer you continue, the more of an impact you will have.

FOCUS YOUR HUNGER

Don't let your craving for results sideline or confuse you. Sure, it would be easier to leave the road or look for a shortcut, but it's worth it to keep pounding the pavement (or the desert, as the case may be). Though hunger could lead you to leave the path, it could lead you to stay too.

The faith of those five thousand–plus people following Jesus was really amazing. They waited it out. Something drove them to see what was at the end of the road. Maybe they needed to be healed, maybe they needed hope, or maybe they knew they might see something incredible happen. They stayed because their hearts were hungry.

> They stayed because their hearts were hungry.

Do we stay for that reason? It is much easier for us to leave the road in search of a quick fix. But that would be like giving up a secret weapon. There's a trick to turning a lack of results into fuel for your mission. How? When you start to get frustrated because you're not seeing things happen, weed and water. Plan and pray. Strategize and ask for support. And continue to dream.

Keep your mind on those veggies. Or that deep-dish pizza. Or that school in Africa. Wait if you have to. And always keep your prayer on. The stalling may just mean that your results will be bigger than you expected. Start to realize that a miracle might be just around the corner. If you give up, you might miss the feeding of the multitudes with your lunch. Remember that food-seeking missile you become when you haven't eaten all day? It's powerful. It's focused. And it can be used for a mission.

STUDY QUESTIONS

1. How can you become a food-seeking missile for Christ? In what way does your hunger lead you toward Him?

2. Do you detect a rumbling in your spiritual stomach? What is it for?

3. What are some of the weirdest things you've eaten because you were starving? What are some things you might substitute for real results?

4. How can you overcome the desire to want to dive into something right away? What are some ways to keep yourself busy while waiting?

5. What do you see as the benefit of running a marathon and not a sprint? How is your journey like one of these two things?

10

The Trader

The sun beat down on us as we walked along the crowded street, looking from left to right at the crazy array of things for sale in the tents and stalls around us. The shouting, the animals, the smells of food, the bustling people, and the sheer variety of stuff packed into those tents almost made me dizzy. I was totally unprepared for our trip to the market in Africa that day. It's not like the mall I'm used to, to say the least!

People were following us around trying to convince us to buy the weirdest stuff. But the art for sale was definitely worth a look—it was amazing. Most of it was handcrafted and coated with shoe polish to bring out the shine. They had tons of wooden carvings of all different kinds of African animals. They're complete tourist-trap items, but I loved them. It's almost unbelievable how each of these aspiring artists can make works of art out of things like discarded metal, plastic, and wire. Each stall was loaded down with unique and creative items, way different from anything I'd seen before in stores in the United States. But the *most* different thing about markets in Africa was the option to trade.

Trading is a lot of fun. I don't know if I enjoyed the fun crafts I bought or the experience of trading more. Vendors are willing to make a trade for just about anything. I have traded everything from socks to rubber bracelets to the shoes on my feet. Money doesn't mean as much as bartering to these folks. In fact, if you hand them too much money, they normally don't have change. They will just try to convince you to buy more from them. Trading has been around for a long time (way before we had money), but sometimes trading can get you stuck in a bad deal. Like trading your car for a pogo stick.

I believe that when it comes to using the gifts and talents God packed in our lunches, there is always an option to trade. There is always that desire. The grass is greener on the other side, they say. It's like the kid in the lunchroom who sees you with a roast beef sandwich and tries to get you to swap it for a bag of greasy chips. As crazy as it sounds, sometimes we fall for it! The trader is the enemy of our soul, as we've mentioned before. And he approaches us in a few different forms. The trader wants us to think that what we have isn't as great as what we could get—that we could get something better if only we would do this or that.

Let's take it back to the Sea of Galilee. As we said earlier, on a road with more than five thousand people, our boy seems to be the only one with a lunch. I don't know about you, but if I saw someone with a lunch after a whole day of walking, I might try to snag it for myself by buying it from him or trading with him. I wonder if this boy was approached by a few people interested in getting him to trade what he had for something different. Maybe something that seemed better—like a nice pair of sandal socks or Pharisee trading cards, or something else that wouldn't exactly make a meal for crowds of hungry followers. The trader gives something in return for your lunch, but what you get is not always that great.

Since the trader has a few different forms, I think we should address those to better prepare ourselves to respond to him. He's sneaky and has many ways to get us to trade, but if we can resist, the results will be so worth the effort it takes to see the bad deal for what it is and turn the trader down.

SNACK-MACHINE SWAPPER

The first way the trader comes at us is by poking holes in our self-confidence and the confidence we have in our gifts. This may not necessarily come in the form of another person demeaning us; it could feel like it's coming from within. Sometimes we get the sinking feeling, seemingly out of nowhere, that we are not capable of having an impact on the world using the tools we have been given.

Let's say you have a baggie full of huge, delicious, homemade chocolate-chip cookies in your lunch—the extra thick and chewy kind with big chocolate chunks—and more than enough to share with your lunch buddies. Plus, they were lovingly made by someone who cares about you and tucked into your lunch with special attention. The trader sniffs you out in the lunchroom. He's got his eye on those cookies and wants to strike a deal for them. In return for your cookies, he tries to offer you a prepackaged snack cake with rubbery icing that probably doesn't even biodegrade. He just got it out of the snack machine; it definitely wasn't made with love. But it has a flashy, glitzy, shiny package. Much fancier than your baggie. He makes a face at your baggie, and you start to wonder . . . could that snack cake be what you're missing? Would your friends be better served if you shared something with them that was store-bought rather than homemade?

Even though the trader never came out and said his cake was better than your cookies, you start to think that way. Often, when we're feeling low about the gifts we have and we don't know where the feeling is coming from, it is coming from Satan (John 8:44). His way of getting us to stop in our tracks? A trade. All of a sudden you might think, *If only God had made me gifted in this other area, I could truly serve Him.*

So how does one go about tackling this ever-growing problem of not feeling that your gifts are enough? There are a couple of ways. The first thing to do is recognize the problem. Recognize the fact that this low self-esteem may not be from you but may have been planted by somebody else. It is natural for us to have doubts at times, but if those doubts are keeping you from moving along the road—if they leave you stuck, scared, and unable to grow—chances are, they are not your own doubts. Call the trader out. Don't let him get away with pretending he's got your best interests at heart. Pray, and ask Jesus to deliver you.

The second way to deal with this lousy kind of trade is to realize what the Creator of the universe promises us: He will never leave us or forsake us (Joshua 1:5). We are forever His. God didn't give us the wrong gifts. No matter how many times we think trading will help us, it doesn't; we've already got top-notch goods. Let's remember and be thankful that God has given us unique gifts, just to us, with care and with love. Your gift is special to you. There's nothing worth trading for something so unique, so one of a kind, as you.

APPETITE STEALER

One of the trader's many disguises is the appetite stealer. He may sit down next to you and start one-upping your lunch: "Oh, man. I just finished the most amazing hot lasagna dinner with all the trimmings." All of a sudden your Uncrustable starts looking a bit puny and unappetizing. The trader says, "Hey, you're not gonna eat the rest of that, are you?" and walks away with your lunch. He just traded your sandwich . . . for an idea! For just the *idea* of a better option. He stole your appetite. These are people who want to downplay your gifts by dissing them or comparing your gifts to theirs.

> There's nothing worth trading for something so unique, so one of a kind, as you.

What do I mean by this? I mean that along the road to making a difference, sometimes you will feel that what you have to offer just doesn't compare. Can you imagine if you were the boy with loaves and fish and you were walking next to the guy who runs the local deli? All of a sudden your lunch might not feel that special. You might feel it's not valuable. You might wish you had a different lunch.

In my first book, *Take Your Best Shot*, I told the story of a boy I met in Africa named George. On my first trip to Zambia, I met George at a church service. I went over to the truck we were riding in and pulled out an old pink soccer ball. We had shoved it into our luggage as an afterthought and didn't see it as anything special. George and I played soccer for a few minutes, and when it was time to go, I gave him the ball. I didn't think much of it. After all, who'd want to lug around an old pink soccer ball? Who knew the difference it would make?

The next day I saw George's mom. She had walked over twelve miles to find me and give me a letter that George had stayed up writing. The letter had a picture of a boy giving another boy a soccer ball. Written in colored pencil across the picture are the words, "Austin and George are friends. I love you very much." Check it out:

This floored me. George and his mom had such big hearts that they went out of their way to give thanks for that old ball. What wonderful people! So I put George's story in *Take Your Best Shot*, and all of a sudden people all over the world were being inspired by George and his mom and this simple sketch. Who knew the kind of impact that George would have just by using his gifts and talents to make a difference? Because George didn't let the gifts of others discourage him, he was able to use what he had to make an impact on his world.

Many times it is easy for us to get overwhelmed by the gifts of others. I always wanted to be a star basketball player when I was younger. But as I grew up, I realized that I wasn't gifted in that area. I was gifted in many unique ways. The same is true for George. His gift was his heart. He didn't get overwhelmed by the thought of being the best soccer player. He realized that he was the best George. He had the best lunch for him—it was made up of a couple of colored pencils and the time it took to write a letter. And it made a huge difference.

I have told the story of George to hundreds of thousands of people now, and they're all blessed by this boy's incredible heart. A little later, I'll tell you about what happened when George's mom was able to see the results of his simple act of giving, but for now let's stick with this first lesson.

If you let others' talents discourage you from using

your own, you might never venture out and use them. If George had not been confident about his colored-pencil skills or his English, he might not have even tried to bless me with that letter. It is so important to realize that you have something amazingly special for the world. If only you are ready to give your lunch, incredible things will happen.

Austin and George

STUDY QUESTIONS

1. Have you ever been tempted to trade one of your spiritual gifts for something "store-bought" or "more appetizing"? When?

2. Where do you see traders in your life? How can you guard against them?

3. Is there something specific that you need to protect from the trader right now? How can you do that?

4. Was there a time when someone in your life really blessed you with something small, like George's letter? What was it? This week, make sure they know what it meant to you, and how their small thing made a big difference.

5. What small thing can you do for someone today?

11

Sandwich Squasher

We've run into a pretty interesting cast of characters so far along the road behind Jesus. Let's add another: the sandwich squasher. I am talking about bullies. You know the type: the kid who shoves people up against the wall of the lunchroom and squashes their sandwiches. Do you think the boy with loaves and fish ran into one of those on the road? My guess is, if teens were the same back then as they are now, the answer is most definitely yes. Our boy probably had to deal with someone like this before and after the miracle. Many of us have probably had to deal with bullies too.

Why does it feel as if these bullies tend to hover around those who are making a difference? What is their fascination with those who try to do good in the world? And how can we deal with the problem? These are the questions I hope to answer in this chapter. I am not an expert on the subject, but I do have firsthand knowledge of it. Bullying has happened to me, and it might happen to you as you work toward using your gifts for God. But there are some great ways to deal with a squasher and get refocused on your purpose, and we're going to talk about them. Just think of them as another way to be prepared for your journey.

WHAT IS BULLYING?

Bullying has been in the news a lot lately. Kids are taking drastic measures and doing some really disturbing stuff. And thanks to TV and the Internet, the problem is more visible than ever before. That's a good thing! Because bullying is one of those problems that we don't want to deal with, but we have to. We've all heard about and witnessed fights breaking out in schoolyards over the degrading words of a bully. But now bullying isn't just in our schoolyards; you can find a bully at school, at church, in the workplace, and sometimes in your own home. Bullying takes place at the highest of levels in the government and the lowest levels of poverty. Bullying is everywhere, every day. But what exactly is bullying? I found this definition on stopbullying.gov:

Bullying can take many forms. Examples include:

- Verbal: name-calling, teasing
- Social: spreading rumors, leaving people out on purpose, breaking up friendships
- Physical: hitting, punching, shoving
- Cyberbullying: using the Internet, mobile phones, or other digital technologies to harm others[1]

Have you experienced anything like this? If you have, can you think back to the situation you were in when it happened? Chances are, yours is one of the situations in which bullying is the most prevalent. That's right: there are certain situations that are pure gold to sandwich squashers—and times when we can even expect to run into a bully.

Why do you think our boy with the lunch may have been picked on? He was doing something out of the ordinary. He was carrying his lunch all the way to the other side of the Sea of Galilee—something nobody else was doing. He was different in that sense. He was special. He was unique. This is an excellent thing—something to be proud of. But a bully may have seen it as a target on his back. The same principle applies to us. If you are making a difference, brace yourself, because you will get picked on.

THE BULLY AND THE BULLIED

For our purposes, let's focus on the bullying that happens to those who serve. I recently conducted a survey that showed some incredible results. Of the people I surveyed, ages ten to fifteen, the majority of those who said they'd been bullied also served in some type of

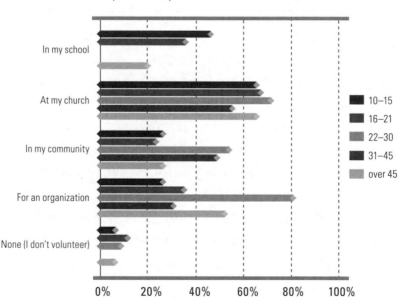

Do you currently serve or volunteer and where?

organization, church, or volunteer service. The same is true for sixteen- to twenty-one-year-olds: 68 percent of them served in some way. When it came to twenty-two- to thirty-year-olds, 81.8 percent served. The breakdown is on the chart on page 142.

One of the first conclusions we can draw from this is that there is a direct correlation between being bullied and serving. I will explain more in just a moment. It goes to show that the more often you are doing good in the world, the higher the chances that you will be bullied. The second conclusion we can draw is that the more often you serve, the more often you are bullied.

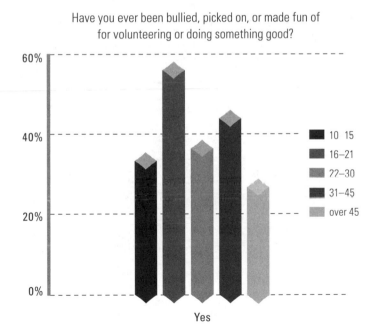

Have you ever been bullied, picked on, or made fun of for volunteering or doing something good?

So if you continually do good in this world, and you do it a lot, you will get bullied a lot. (Don't worry! We'll get to some solutions in a minute.) The third conclusion we can draw is the age range of people being bullied for serving is on the young side. Take a look at those statistics one more time. You notice that the age range sixteen- to twenty-one-year-olds has the highest incidents of bullying.

The most bullied people on this graph (page 143) are young people like us. We get picked on for doing good more than other age groups. Why? Maybe bullies just grow out of their bullying ways. Maybe they start to realize that doing good is, in fact, good. Instead of picking on someone for serving, maybe they recognize the value of serving and start to do it themselves.

WHY?

A question I hoped to answer through the survey is the question of why. Why do bullies tend to target those who serve? I posed this question to the participants of my survey: "Why do you believe you were bullied, picked on, or made fun of for volunteering?" Out of all the age groups, sixteen- to twenty-one-year-olds gave the most responses. I think this is because we have the most recent, firsthand experience. Take a look at some of the amazing answers I received from all age groups:

- "Because, at times, it is hard for others to fully understand why you do what you do." (ages 16–21)
- "Either because someone didn't understand what I was volunteering for or because they wanted my time." (ages 16–21)
- "Other people are unsatisfied with their own level of volunteering, or uncomfortable with confronting some of the issues that volunteering can support." (ages 16–21)
- "Jealousy or my actions made others feel intimidated or threatened." (ages over 45)
- "Because others want to belittle you out of a lack of self-esteem." (ages 31–45)
- "Because the people bullying didn't understand why I was doing it and why I kept doing it even after the bullying." (ages 22–30)
- "Because in their eyes it wasn't the cool thing to do." (ages 10–15)
- "Other people see me as a 'goody-two-shoes.' Many times, though, I think it is because of their own insecurity." (ages 16–21)

When I read through these responses for the first time, I thought, *Wow*. This list of responses goes on and on, and each one is incredibly insightful. People really seem to get what the root of the problem is.

I believe that the answer to the question of *why* is

pretty specific to each person's situation, but there are some common characteristics of a bully. I'm very familiar with what they are because I was bullied from junior high to my junior year in high school. It is tough. It is something I didn't like, but if I hadn't gone through it, I don't think I could have convincingly written this chapter or helped those going through it themselves. I would have no place telling you how to handle a bully. But I have had a pretty intense life experience in this area for five years. I believe that God allowed me to go through that so I could help others.

I have found that bullies tend to bully those making a difference for three main reasons.

They don't understand what you are doing.

Sandwich squashers might not get why you want to make a difference or why you seem to care about others. You seem different to them. This boy in the miracle may have seemed different because he was the only one carrying a lunch. When you are the only one making a difference, it may seem disturbingly unusual or scary to some. The inability to understand what's going on can make some people frustrated and angry, leading them to take it out on others. I experienced bullying for this reason many times. People who picked on and made fun of me didn't really understand why I would leave to go speak on the weekends. They didn't understand Hoops of Hope. Because of that, I was bullied. All because they didn't understand.

They feel threatened.

Deep down, perhaps bullies really do care about making a difference. They feel a little threatened by the fact that others are doing something that they wish they were doing. It can come down to an actual sense of jealousy. They might be jealous of what you are doing and the impact you are making on the world. They might be jealous of the positive attention you receive. They might feel bad about themselves and secretly think you are a great person, so they offset those feelings by bullying you. This one is a little bit harder to understand, but I think it is true. It has been said many times that a bully is really just insecure about him- or herself. Understanding that your bully may be jealous of you can be very surprising, but it makes a lot of sense.

They think it will make them look better.

If you're dealing with jealous bullies, you can see how they may be picking on you to make themselves look better. They wish they were making a difference (because making a difference is very cool), so they try to push you down in order to push themselves up. Say, for instance, that you're looking at a large tree. You are represented by a high branch, and a branch beneath you is your "bully branch." The bully pulls the tip of the tree down so the top branch is lower than the bully branch. Now the bully's is the highest branch on the tree. It isn't really the highest branch, but it looks like it. In this same sense, bullies may come after you because they want to look better than you. The only way they can think of to look better is to push you down. This is one of the worst forms of bullying.

AM I BEING BULLIED?

So how exactly do you recognize when you are being bullied? Sure, sometimes it may be obvious, like when someone is physically beating you up or constantly tearing you down with insults. But other times it's harder to tell.

There is a difference between a friendly joust of words and verbal bullying. Most of the time, if your "friendly joust" is going both ways, it's safe to say the person really likes you and isn't trying to put you down. But there is a very fine line between playing and serious. I once had a friend who was great to be around when it was just the two of us, but really difficult to be around when there were more people. His words got more and more negative toward me, and it turned into intentional bullying.

Another subtle way of bullying is making sure you

don't feel accepted in a group. This is another thing I actually experienced firsthand. From guys. You may think this is a girl thing to do, but this kind of subtle bullying spans all age groups and both genders. You have to recognize it when it comes. And if you remember the chapter on fear, not being accepted is a fear of 84 percent of sixteen- to twenty-one-year-olds and a fear in 60 percent of all age groups. Making us feel unaccepted is one of the most common ways bullies can really get to us. They might spread rumors about us or badmouth us to our friends behind our backs, making us feel isolated and unloved. It's a dirty move. It is also an unseen move many times. But despite all the sneaky and not-so-sneaky ways of a bully, just remember, the road isn't supposed to be easy. If it were, everyone would take it.

One of the newest weapons in a bully's arsenal is the Internet. Of course the Internet is awesome, but it also makes it easy for someone to disguise him- or herself and take jabs at people. This kind of behavior is called cyberbullying. Cyberbullying is a new and cowardly way to try to hurt someone while hiding behind a mask online. It can be anything from leaving a mean comment on someone's Facebook page to intentionally posting an embarrassing photo of someone in order to make fun of them to hacking into a target's personal accounts in an attempt to hurt their reputation. Sometimes bullies feel free to be even crueler and say more hurtful things online that they would not say to your face. Cyberbullies, anonymous or not, can be some of the worst bullies, so watch out for them and don't be afraid to take action.

SOLUTIONS FOR BULLYING

So how exactly can we deal with bullies? We now have a good understanding of why and how they do what they do, but how do we stop it?

There are all sorts of ways people will tell you to deal with this. Throughout my years of being bullied, I tried every trick in the book. Some worked and some didn't. So let me tell you about what worked for me.

Pray

Some might say, "Fight fire with fire." I have tried that one, and it doesn't work. It just makes a bigger fire. If you hurl back an insult at someone who is bad-mouthing you, the anger just grows, and things get worse. Instead, the first and most important way to deal with bullies is to pray for them. It may sound easy, but, honestly, it is one of the hardest things a person can do. Matthew 5:44 says, "Love your enemies and pray for those who persecute you." When you are praying for people who persecute you, you are forgiving them before they have even asked for forgiveness. That is an amazing and holy thing. Why? Because "while we were still sinners, Christ died for us" (Romans 5:8). We hadn't even thought about asking for forgiveness, but He gave it to us, and because of that we are able to live in freedom and be close to God.

A bully can really harm your spiritual life. That is why it is so important to pray for that person. Every day. I would also encourage you to pray for a renewed spirit.

> "Love your enemies and pray for those who persecute you."

Pray that God will continue to renew your spirit and keep your head up high. This has helped me many times to look at that person and love as Christ does instead of harboring bitterness in my heart.

Bring in Backup

Another way to deal with a bully is to tell an adult. Personally I believe there would be much less bullying in this world if adults didn't take a backseat to it. When you are being bullied in school, talk to a teacher you trust. I was actually bullied by a teacher throughout school. I ended up having to switch to an online course because this teacher was such a verbal bully. So make sure you're going to someone you can really trust. Don't feel as though you're being a tattletale; you have to make a teacher aware of what is happening.

Teachers have the job of putting an end to bullying

in the school system. It's their job to keep order around a school. I can honestly say that if teachers had stepped up on many occasions, I would not have gone through the kind of torture I did. Teachers not only *should* step in; they have the *responsibility* to step in. This may come across as harsh, but I believe that if teachers cared more about this aspect of their classroom than being liked, this world would be better place. If bullying is stopped at an early age, it doesn't continue to grow.

If you are a student, stand up for your fellow students. Come to their defense, but get help from an authority figure. Whether you are a senior in high school or a first grader, get help from others. But here is the sad thing: a recent study found that only 14 percent of teachers intervene in bullying incidents inside the classroom.[2] If you are a teacher reading this, I would encourage you to talk to your students about the issue of bullying and put a stop to it the second it arises. If you are a parent, even if your child hasn't had to deal with bullying, I would encourage you to educate yourself and talk with your principals and teachers about the issue. It would save so many kids from being bullied if only an adult got involved.

Reach Out to a Bully

It is important to remember that changing the world comes with a cost. It sometimes comes with a few very difficult challenges. The next time someone tries to bully you because you are making a difference, try this. Invite that person to serve with you. It may sound scary and crazy. But I have tried it, and those same people who bullied me eventually started showing up at Hoops of Hope events. It may not mend the relationship, but if they do serve, they will better understand what you do. It may even stop the bullying.

••••◆•••••

All in all, bullying is a much bigger problem than most people ever think it is. Bullying can leave scars that may last a lifetime. If bullying were taken out of the world, we would have much fewer suicides, much less depression, and much happier people. If only we would recognize the problem and deal with it God's way. In John 6, our boy probably had to go through some challenging stuff to give his lunch to Jesus, especially on the long and crowded road (check out Luke 18:15–17 to see how children were sometimes treated during those days, even by Jesus' own disciples). In the same way, you may have to take on a few difficult challenges. So when you do, remember that if following Jesus were easy, everyone would do it. The Bible says that few make it down the narrow road. Those few are an elite group that may have to go through a season of bullying. But those who stay on the road, even through struggles, are so much more equipped to serve God. So stay on the road.

My final encouragement on this topic is to remember the words of Paul. Paul was beaten, stoned, and thrown in prison by his own people, yet he had this to say in 1 Corinthians 4:12: "When we are cursed, we bless; when we are persecuted, we endure it."

Sometimes you must endure the torture of a bully. Many find the road, but few reach the end of it. Reach the end.

LETTER TO A SANDWICH SQUASHER

Maybe you just finished reading through this chapter and you realized, *I might be a bully!* Take a look back at those definitions at the beginning of the chapter. Do any of those fit you? If so, you probably are. It is pretty easy for us to want to deny something rather than realize it is true. If you are a bully, there is still so much hope for you. My encouragement to you is to do a few different things:

1. Realize that you are a bully. Own it. Understand it. But don't let it define you. No longer are you a bully; you *were* a bully. Admit that you have done wrong and move on.

2. The most important thing someone who was a bully can do is ask for forgiveness. It might be

the hardest thing in the entire world to do, but I can guarantee you that the person you have hurt will think so much more of you. You have the chance to renew that person's spirit.

I actually received a Facebook message while we were editing this chapter. It was from someone who had bullied me every day during my junior year of high school. Someone who would bully me with her words and her looks, and she even drew ugly pictures on the classroom board daily and wrote my name under them. Guess what? She wrote me an e-mail asking for forgiveness. It is one of the most incredible things someone has ever done for me. A simple message telling me I was a great person and saying she was so sorry for everything she had put me through. She wasn't the only one who bullied me. I doubt I will ever receive a message like that again, but I was so thankful to God for it. It brought peace and closure to that situation. It made forgiveness real. I forgive because I am forgiven, and though I had forgiven that person long ago, her note meant a lot and was such a gift to me.

If you can ask for forgiveness, you can ease the hurt that the person you harmed is feeling. You have the chance to have an amazing impact in that way. It is the most important thing you can do after realizing you have been a bully.

3. Lastly, pray and ask God for forgiveness. I would encourage you to tell God what you are feeling. He listens. Let Him know how sorry you are. And begin praying for those you have hurt.

If you do these things, you are on your way to becoming one of the nicest people ever. You will become a friend to all. I want to become your friend. And you'll have gotten rid of something that could keep you from using your own gifts. Sometimes fixing the hurt you have caused can even be a way of bringing out those spiritual gifts.

There's an amazing example from the Bible that you may not be aware of. It's Paul. Yep, the same Paul who gave us so much wisdom about enduring persecution. The apostle who helped spread Christianity around the world. The one who spent his waking hours in prison writing and encouraging churches. Before all that, *he* was a bully. A big, horrible bully. You can read the whole story in Acts 9. Back in his bully days, Paul was called Saul. He spent his time hunting down Christians, "breathing out murderous threats against the Lord's disciples" (v. 1).

But then Jesus came to him in a vision along the road to Damascus, asking, "Saul, Saul, why do you persecute me?" (v. 4). Saul was knocked off his donkey and struck blind, shocked to learn that Jesus was Lord, and that He had a plan for someone like him. With the help of Ananias (a Christian whom God sent to help Saul—and who was pretty nervous at first about working with such a bully), Saul was transformed into Paul, God's "chosen instrument" (v. 15). It's an amazing story! And God still transforms people today. So begin your own walk along the road, and reach the end with strength, grace, and your head held high.

STUDY-QUESTIONS

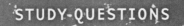

1. HOW DOES BULLYING AFFECT YOU PERSONALLY? CAN YOU NAME A TIME WHEN YOU WERE BULLIED?
2. HOW HAS IT AFFECTED THOSE AROUND YOU? WHAT WERE THESE SITUATIONS LIKE?
3. HAVE YOU EVER BEEN A BULLY? IF SO, HOW CAN YOU MAKE THINGS RIGHT?
4. IF YOU ARE EVER BULLIED OR WITNESS BULLYING, WHO IS AN ADULT YOU CAN TRUST TO HELP? THINK OF WAYS YOU CAN BE PREPARED.
5. HOW CAN YOU PUT A STOP TO BULLYING IN YOUR LIFE AND THE LIVES OF OTHERS?

Give It

If I had the choice to be present for one of Jesus' miracles, I would choose the miracle of the loaves and fish. I guess you could tell that by now! We have envisioned it many times throughout this book and explored the ways it can teach you about your special gifts. I hope that the picture I have painted of what happened on that day is as clear as possible for you. The boy has walked along the road with fear, deserters, traders, and sandwich squashers, all to make it to the final place—the chance to give his lunch. A 19.3-mile journey along a bumpy road has reached its destination. It feels good to finally be here! The chance to give it all has arrived.

Jesus stands in front of the massive crowd. The boy can see Him up there teaching. Then it begins; the people begin to stand and grumble because of hunger. A disciple finds the boy and asks him if he has a lunch to share. Does he ever! He gives away the lunch he so carefully protected along the road. Jesus takes those two fish and five small barley loaves, prays to God, and then the disciples start handing them out. Every last one of the people are fed—by the young boy's lunch. Incredible!

But let's rewind just a little bit. What two things were necessary for this whole thing to happen? What two thoughts had to go through the boy's head before he handed over his lunch? Right at the moment of truth, when the disciples came around asking for food, the kid could have waffled around and avoided them, missing his chance. Or he could have stuffed a few loaves in his mouth for himself before handing the rest over. But instead he had two amazing impulses: *give it now* and *give it all*. How freeing it must have been to watch what happened when he did just that!

GIVE IT NOW

Sometimes when it comes right down to the defining moment, we begin to ask ourselves, *Why can't I just do something later? I'm way too busy right now. Why can't*

I take care of a few things and then give my gifts in a few minutes? Or tomorrow? Or next week?

So why can't we? The truth is, we can wait until later. But chances are we won't follow through. People tend to put off "doing something with their life" because, well, "I'm in school right now." Or "I'm way too focused on all my afterschool activities." Or some other thing. If we think about it, there is never going to be a time when we aren't busy doing something. We're in school right now, then we're busy with college, then we're busy with a job, and then, well, we have a family. The list goes on. We are always going to be busy and feel like we don't have time to do something bigger than ourselves. So do it now! Nowhere does God say, "You need to have a degree to make a difference." Not once.

I think every one of us has met an adult who has said, "I wish I knew what I know now when I was your age." What they are trying to say is that they didn't know they *could* do something then. And now, because of that lack of empowerment, the bar is set a lot lower for our generation. It is odd to me how we are not expected to do good things as teenagers. It seems to blow us away when we hear about a kid making a difference. Think about young people like Anne Frank—or even Alexander the Great or Joan of Arc or David. Seems unbelievable what they did as young people, right? But why all the excitement? Why do these kinds of things rarely happen for us?

The bar is set *so* low that the best people can expect of us is to not do drugs, to get good grades, to not drink, to not have sex before marriage . . . and the list ends about there. Really? Our generation can do so much more. We were *meant* to do so much more. When we're older, we can be the ones who say, "I'm glad I knew what I now know when I was younger." And we can start today. We can turn the tide on this belief of waiting until we're older to make a mark on the world for Christ.

So when you get to the point on the road where you ask yourself, *Why can't I put this off a little?* try to think of a really good reason to use your lunch today. People need our help now, and we can help them. Our generation is taking a step up each year. It is our time to shine. We can turn the tide on the problems of this world. But not just someday. Not in a little while. We can turn the tide on those problems *now*. In Christ, we have the power to do it. So to our generation I say, let's not let an issue of being too busy hold us back; let's make a difference today.

GIVE IT ALL

This boy was all in. He gave everything he had to Jesus, and it was hard-core. There was no sneaking, no wimping out, and no holding back. That's why I'm so impressed with him. As far as we know, he didn't keep anything for himself. He wasn't suspicious that these twelve guys would swipe his lunch and leave him hungry. I mean, he had carried the thing for so far, wouldn't you think he deserved to have a little bit of it on his own? He totally could have taken a few bites first. But the Bible doesn't talk about a half-eaten fish or a loaf with a mouth-shaped chunk missing from it. It's amazing to think that this boy didn't want to eat a little bit of it. I honestly would have. But he clearly had faith—or was so amazed by the fact that Jesus was going to use his lunch—that he just gave everything he had. What a concept.

For us, the same exact thing applies; it takes faith. Not a little bit of faith but a ton of it. It's faith that God gives us Himself.

Giving it all can be hard at times. It isn't exactly the easiest thing to want to give everything you have—but we have to. What happens if someone goes out and plays in the World Cup at 50 percent? He will be pulled from the game in a heartbeat. The same is true for us. We aren't going to be pulled from the game, of course, but if we truly want to have an impact, if we truly want to change the world for Christ, it's important to open up our hands and give our gifts and talents to God. When Christ died for you and me on the cross, He gave His all.

When you are ready to make a difference, give it everything you've got. Just give it. The results are so much more powerful when we're totally invested in what we are doing. It's this commitment, not necessarily talent or natural ability or other advantages, that really makes an impact. So when you give it, put all your power behind it and just see what God does.

ENOUGH

So Jesus took the lunch, and it was enough to "feed everyone." It was Him! He did it! There was no reason to look at that little snack and think it would be enough. That's what the miracle was all about. The concept of "enough" can be a doubt that can threaten us at the very crucial hour. Right when we are about to make a difference, we might not move because of this doubt. Imagine a double-take. We look at the problem we're trying to solve and then we look back at ourselves and then we look at the problem again. Not much by comparison, is it? We realize that we are looking straight up at a hundred-foot wall that, from a distance, had seemed small enough for us to jump over. All of a sudden we realize how big the problem is compared to how small we are.

I have felt this at a few different points with Hoops of Hope. Hoops of Hope set out to help those affected by HIV/AIDS. But the problem is that there are more than 15 million children orphaned because of this disease. To put that picture into perspective, if those 15 million kids were to link hands and stretch in a single line, they would go from New York to Los Angeles and back again five and a half times! That problem has turned into that hundred-foot wall, daring us to even try to knock it down. And all we have in our hand is a chisel. Or at least that is what it feels like.

But that chisel can do things to that wall that you wouldn't believe. That chisel can slowly but surely bring that wall down to size. It can bring it down to our level. It sounds crazy, because a chisel has never really brought down a wall—but with the help of God it can.

Sometimes the problem you want to solve can seem like a huge thing, made of stone, but if you are persistent enough to make a dent, you are having an impact. We don't have to tear the whole wall down ourselves. We can do our part by chiseling at the wall. It's more about doing each of our parts than bringing down the wall by ourselves.

Think about the story of Jericho. Why did that wall come down in Joshua 6? Joshua 6:20 says, "When the trumpets sounded, the army shouted, and at the sound of the trumpet, when the men gave a loud shout, the wall collapsed; so everyone charged straight in, and they took the city." It wasn't one guy shouting; it was all of them shouting.

The same thing is true with the wall of Berlin. The world was shouting against injustices in Germany, and Ronald Reagan said something too. They are words etched into our minds, spoken by one of my favorite leaders.

He said, "Mr. Gorbachev, tear down this wall!" There is no longer a wall dividing Germany. The symbol of communism was torn down in favor of the freedom our country holds so dear. The wall did not come down right after his speech. The wall came down more than two years later. But the wall came down. And freedom rings.

Also take comfort in the fact that you're not going up against the wall by yourself. Imagine that hundred-foot wall with our entire generation chiseling at it. It will come down pretty quickly. If each of us does a little part, we can solve the major problems facing our world. If America alone didn't spend any money on ice cream this year, we could solve the problem of world hunger and many other diseases (including America's growing obesity problem!). Want a simple way to chisel? Every time you would normally go out for ice cream, put that money in a jar, and at the end of the year, donate it. Even a few bucks can make a difference to those desperately in need.

There's a great story I like to tell about the difference a little bit can make. It's the story of the boy and the starfish.

Early one morning a boy was walking along a beach when he came upon thousands of starfish washed up on the shore. He felt compassion for these starfish, so one by one, he bent down, picked up a starfish, and threw it back into the sea. He did it as fast as he could, but the beach was still covered with starfish.

Soon an older man came jogging by, and he asked the boy, "What are you doing?" The boy said, "I'm trying to save these starfish." The man said, "You can't possibly make a difference for all these starfish! There are thousands of them on this beach." Then the little boy bent down, picked one up, and threw it into the sea. He looked the man in the eye, held up his small finger, and said, "I made a difference for that one."

Whether you are making a difference for thousands, just chiseling, or throwing starfish one by one, your actions make a difference. You are making an impact on the wall. Eventually, that wall will be torn down because you and people like you cared and decided to do something. Even if you never see it come down yourself, you've done your part—and you will always have the power to make a difference for one. Never forget that. Plus, God will never leave us or forsake us. He won't leave us in front of that wall with our chisels, nor will He leave us in the corner of the lunchroom.

As you are walking up to the crowd with those spiritual gifts in hand, remember the things we talked about in this chapter. Give your all, give it now, and know it's enough. Instead of waiting around for someone else to take a stand, just do it. Do it and watch as thousands of others join you with their chisels along the wall. You can be the start of something big, if you are ready to give your lunch.

STUDY QUESTIONS

1. WHAT WOULD "GIVING IT ALL" LOOK LIKE TO YOU?

2. IF YOU COULD DO ANYTHING FOR GOD, REGARDLESS OF HOW HARD IT IS OR WHAT IT WOULD TAKE, WHAT WOULD THAT BE?

3. HAVE YOU EVER HAD THE FEELING OF GIVING YOUR ALL TO SOMETHING AND "LEAVING IT ALL ON THE FIELD"? TELL ABOUT THAT TIME AND HOW IT MADE YOU FEEL.

4. IS THERE ANYTHING KEEPING YOU FROM "GIVING IT NOW"?

5. WHAT HUGE WALL ARE YOU LOOKING AT? HOW CAN YOU CHISEL TODAY?

13

The Results

As we talked about earlier, God doesn't need you. God didn't need that boy. God doesn't need me. If God had wanted to, He could have fed those five thousand hungry people just by thinking the thought. He is powerful enough to end AIDS, hunger, the national debt, wars, natural disasters, and every problem we see, just like that! But by now, you have an idea of why He doesn't. That's right—He wants to use us. He doesn't need to, but He takes incredible joy in using us to do good in the world. And when we allow God to use us, the results are amazing—for those affected, for ourselves, and for the people around us.

A ROUGH ROAD THAT LEADS TO JOY

There's someone else in the Bible who got to see some shockingly amazing results in his lifetime. His name was Elijah. And we're talking huge, crazy, movie-special-effects-level results. The kind that knock you on your back and burn your eyebrows off . . . literally. But the thing was, Elijah had a pretty tough time using his spiritual gift. That gift—the assignment given to him by God—was communicating to the wicked king Ahab what God had to say about his evil actions. It was a rough road that ended up getting Elijah almost killed on a few occasions and had him running for his life in others. You could say he faced some extreme bullying of biblical proportions.

You see, Elijah was a man of God. There were only a few in the entire country. Talk about lonely. But Elijah stayed on the narrow road. He ended up having to depend on God to be fed by ravens and by the last food of a widow. Can you imagine having to have faith for each meal? Not knowing where it was coming from but believing it would come? Elijah did it day in and day out. It was a road full of all of the bumps we have talked about in previous chapters and more. But Elijah didn't take it for nothing. He got to see a miracle happen firsthand.

Imagine this. At his moment of truth—the moment God

called Elijah to give his all and hold nothing back—he was surrounded by 450 false prophets of Baal. He had led the Israelites up to meet those 450 irritable guys on top of a mountain, where they had arranged a face-off between their false god and the God of Israel. Elijah patiently waited as the prophets tried every trick in the book to show that their god was real. All the false prophets wanted Baal to do was take their offering of a bull. They called out to their god all day long, singing and dancing and shouting and begging for fire, and even going so far as to slash themselves with knives to let their god know they were there. As you probably guessed, nothing happened. Nothing at all. Their bull just sat there on the table waiting to be taken.

Elijah, on the other hand, patiently waited his turn while the prophets continued to put on a show. Elijah knew his rough road hadn't been for nothing, and his faith wasn't for nothing either. He wanted the people of Israel to know without a doubt that God is the one true God and there is no other god in the world but Him. So Elijah took the competition to a whole new level. He completely soaked the offering in water three times. He went as far as to fill a trench surrounding the offering area full of water. It seemed impossible that fire could even singe one of the bull's hairs, let alone burn it all up. Then Elijah backed away and prayed. Next, he looked up and watched the results. First Kings 18:38 says:

Then the fire of the LORD fell and burned up the sacrifice, the wood, the stones and the soil, and also licked up the water in the trench.

Boom! Another miracle I wish I'd been present for. God extravagantly proved that He was God and these were His people. He went overboard—just as He did later when He was pumping out leftovers at the feast of the five thousand. It was awesome. Elijah may have lost his eyebrows that day, but, boy, did he get to see the results! Elijah didn't do it; God did. God showed His power and used Elijah in His miracle.

YOUR RESULTS

God has prepared miracles to use you for—miracles just as amazing as fire falling from heaven. So walk the road and watch the results. The results that day by the Sea of Galilee were stunning: thousands of people were fed and praising God. And why did this miracle happen that way? Because a little boy used what he had been given to change the world. He walked the 19.3 miles, gave his lunch to the One who could do something with it, and wasn't intimidated by the ratio between his small snack and the number of hungry people. One boy decided to just *do* something. And God in the flesh decided to use a small boy that day to show His glory to the world.

For me, the opportunity to see God's glory like this has come around a few times in my life so far. I've seen it on the faces of students able to go to high school for the first time—and on the faces of adults who would be able to go to night school and get an education. I have had the chance to visit Africa five times now, and each time I see what kinds of things happen when people around the world use their gifts to make a difference. At the opening of the Jonathan Sim Legacy High School in Zambia, I knew it was an experience I'd never forget—it was stamped into my heart. All the hard work and rough roads people had taken to raise the money and build the school were so worth it. On all of their faces, I read joy. I think it's the kind of joy we share with God when something like a miracle happens before our eyes.

Now, a few years after the school opened, it seems as if this crazy miracle continues. On a previous trip to Zambia, I met with some of the students who are attending the school. They are getting better grades than some of the students going to schools in the city! They are learning and growing in ways they never knew possible. What's next for them? The sky is the limit. Hoops of Hope was able to fund four dorms at the school a few years back, so students who have never slept in a bed are able to for the very first time. Students who had never seen a computer are now able to teach their fellow students how to use one in the newly constructed computer lab.

Students who never have felt water fall from a shower-head don't have to worry about keeping clean anymore. The results are overwhelming; and, like the butterfly effect, they'll keep going. When you step out and make a difference, the results might just blow you away.

GEORGE'S MOM: SHARING THE RESULTS

It was June of 2010, on a scorching day in southern Zambia. It seemed as if the sun had come a little closer to earth that day so we would remember it was still there. We sang, danced, listened, and spoke for the dedication of the four brand-new dorms at the Jonathan Sim Legacy School in Zambia. It was a great day of celebration and joy. My days in Africa are some of my fondest for that reason. And for this reason.

While I was walking across the schoolyard, a woman came up to me. She called out my name and came running to meet me. She shook my hand. Her face looked familiar, but I couldn't quite put my finger on it. Not until she said this: "My name is Charity, and I have a son named George. The last time you were here, you gave my son a soccer ball. I know you probably don't remember him or know who he is, but he told me to tell you hi."

My jaw wanted to fall right off. In a millisecond, my brain was trying to process the idea that this was actually

George's mom. I couldn't believe that she was standing right in front of me. I know that I fumbled for my next words as I said, "Yes, of course I remember your son!"

The next few hours were spent in joyful conversation with George's mom. I told her all about how much of a hero her son was to me. I told her about how I travel and speak about her son. I told her about the five hundred thousand people who must know his story by now. I even showed her the chapter about George in my first book. The chapter is called "One Pink Soccer Ball." I couldn't believe that this was happening! But then again, neither could she. It was a struggle for her to get her head around it too. She was really trying to take in what a difference her son had made, and her tears of joy hinted that she understood the situation. Then she got it: her son had lived to give.

You'll remember from earlier in the book that George wrote a short little thank-you letter about how much it meant to him that I gave him a soccer ball. That short little letter has helped me encourage people all across the world that when you help change someone else's life, it changes yours! George could have not said anything; after all, it was just an old, beat-up soccer ball. Instead he made a huge

When you help change someone else's life, it changes yours!

difference through his letter that encouraged me and others around the world!

So don't keep the results to yourself. Let others see them. God doesn't need us; He wants us.

CHANGED

Thinking about George's mom makes me think about what the little boy's mom must have felt when her son came home from witnessing a miracle by the Sea of Galilee. That's probably the kind of moment that every parent would love to have with his or her child. Imagine her seeing her boy come home and hearing how his simple lunch had been used by Jesus to do such a miracle. Talk about proud!

Maybe she had woken up that morning and told her child about how he should go see Jesus. She convinced him and he decided to try to hear Jesus teach. The mom pointed at a neatly packed lunch on the table, and then she sent her child off. Late that evening, the boy came bursting through the door with a smile from ear to ear. Before she could even utter a word, he said, "I met Jesus today in an incredible way!"

When we have seen the results, the most important thing is for us to realize that we have met Jesus in an incredible way. Making a difference is a huge high for all of us. Whether it is a massive Hoops of Hope event or something as simple as giving a few dollars to a homeless man, it all has a deep impact on us. We feel a sudden surge of gratitude and joy. We realize that we have made a difference for others, and therefore it makes a difference in us. It's Jesus working in us. When we see Him at work—using our lunches to make a difference, all while making us more like Him—we're changed in ways we never thought possible. He lived to give, and when we do the same, we start feeling what it's like to really live.

It's a simple truth that changing someone else's life always changes yours. This was so true for me when I met George for the first time. My life was forever changed from that encounter with him. Sure, the soccer ball I gave George eventually went flat, but the letter he sent never will. The lessons and memories I got from George and his mom will last a lifetime.

GROWING THROUGH GIVING

My mom once said something very inspiring to me. She said, "People always say that God doesn't put us into something we can't handle. But I think that sometimes He does. He puts us into something we can't handle so we can grow to handle it."

Wow! That's another way that living to give actually gives back to us. We grow. Remember one of my favorite verses, Romans 8:28? God promises that *all* things work together for the good of those who love Him. As my mom pointed out, especially the hard things.

We sometimes ask why God would put us in a certain situation: it might be anything from struggling to meet a deadline to fighting against extreme injustice or a deadly disease. We claim that we can't handle it. Guess what? We could be right. Many times we can't handle it. Only God can.

In those times when we can't handle it, we feel as though we're in a smoke-filled room, making a run for the exit sign. Things might be burning around us, but God gently puts a hand out. We latch onto it. But then it gets worse, so He puts His arm around us. When we get dizzy and it looks like the exit sign is fading away, God snatches us into His arms and walks. He takes off His oxygen mask and hands it up to us. He walks us through the difficult situation step by step. He lets us see the exit sign while we're on His shoulders. We cling to the hope of how close we are. But each step God takes makes us stronger because we are learning to depend more on the One who saves us. Giving in to God actually builds us up spiritually.

Then, bursting forth into the light, we break out of the smoky room. God gently sets us back on our feet. Instead of walking away to the waiting fire truck, He continues to walk with us. Instead of saying good-bye and promising to come back and help us the next time we find ourselves in a fire, He walks next to us all the way home. Even if it means passing through a couple more smoke-filled rooms.

Whether your smoky room is you trying to make a difference, a hard day at school, or an emotionally difficult time, I would encourage you to let God carry you. Let Him. It's a two-way road; God is always going to hold out His arms for us, but we have to be willing to let Him carry us. God is always right by us, ready help us out and hand us the oxygen. The oxygen for us is His Word. You'll remember one of my favorite promises in Hebrews 13:5: "God has said, 'Never will I leave you; never will I forsake you.'" And then there's another promise from Jesus in Matthew 6:26: "Look at the birds of the air; they do not sow or reap or store away in barns, and yet your heavenly Father feeds them. Are you not much more valuable than they?"

Jesus cared enough about the people around Him going hungry that He picked up the crowd and carried them in a big way. Jesus cared and still cares about you and me today. Whenever you have anything hard come up along your road, He's got you! God doesn't take promises lightly—God will keep them. I am so thankful for promises like that. They make the smoke-filled rooms of life more breathable.

The end of the road holds amazing moments for all

of us. It can be a long road or a very short one, but nevertheless, living to give will change us and change others—and the road will be filled with unbelievable moments of grace from God. But on the hard parts of the road and the happiest parts of the road, let's thank God that He is with us, and remember that we could never do this without Him.

STUDY QUESTIONS

1. What do the results of giving look like for you? If they haven't happened yet, can you envision them?
2. Can you remember a time when your life was changed by giving? How did it change you?
3. How can that experience inspire you as you continue to give your gifts to God?
4. When has God carried you through a "smoke-filled room"?
5. Can you think of a time when someone sharing their results with you energized you? Or when you did that for someone else? What was it like?

14

Our World

This book is called *Live to Give* for a reason. It is not *Live to Make a Difference Once and Be Done with It*. First off, that is way too long of a title to fit on the front of the book. But more important, a title like that would lead you astray. Living to give is a way of life. There's a tendency in our culture to think that making a difference or even giving is just checking off one to-do item after another, graduating from thing to thing. Birth, check. Preschool, check. First grade, first dance, first job, first car, first love, first kid, the list goes on. Giving is sometimes made out as a checkbox on the list of life.

If we check the box every week with our tithes, we don't have to worry about it until next week. Tithes are, of course, a necessary way to help our local church, but we can do so much more. We can give things that money can't buy: our talents, our time, our love and enthusiasm, our lives! We are called to do more. Luke 12:48 basically says, "Great gifts mean great responsibilities; greater gifts, greater responsibilities!"

I honestly don't want us to ever feel guilty about being given great gifts, even here in the United States, where things tend to come a little easier than in other places. We have the opportunity to live in one of the greatest countries on the earth. We have been given much, thank God! So we are required to do something with that.

After having read about some people who have lived to give, and after being prepared for what it might be like for you to take that step, I hope that this "requirement" seems overwhelmingly exciting to you. I hope it's like someone telling you that you are now "required" to do your absolute favorite thing in the world as much as you want, "required" to see it bring joy and help to others, and "required" to hang out with God and celebrate the results. And you are required to pass this book on to a friend! Life is tough. But really, even though there are bumps and bruises that may discourage you or try to stop you in your tracks, they make you stronger, they teach you to rely on God, and they make for a great story.

That story is the start of a lifetime of stories. I wish the Bible had told us about the rest of the boy's adventures after Jesus multiplied his loaves and fish. Something tells me it was just the beginning for him, and that the miracle by the Sea of Galilee was only one of the many stories he told his grandkids by the fire when he was older. God's love for the boy went far beyond that one-time chance to give his lunch to Jesus. That boy's legacy was more than just fish and bread. The same is true for us.

When you're older, what stories do you hope to tell? How will your gifts and favorite things translate into stories to be passed down through the generations? What do you want to be remembered for? Even better, what *will* you be remembered for?

Are you and God writing those stories together now? As you can probably tell, I want to tell my grandkids stories about Africa—about George, the faces of the students at the school, the lives saved by the clinic, and about all sorts of people and events that will take place in the future.

For Christians, the greatest collection of stories to pass down is written in the Bible. It's up to you how you choose to add your stories to those of Elijah and David and the kid with the bread and fish. But the greatest example of living to give is the story God Himself—of His Son. Jesus' story is the ultimate story—and the accounts of His miracles are an amazing collection that God loves to tell His kids. The absolute, undisputed highlight, the biggest, most amazing story of all—and the one we stake our lives on—is the one about the time Jesus died. And came back to life. For us. There is nothing that beats that.

Jesus' whole purpose for coming to earth was to give His life for us. The Bible says in Mark 10:45, "Even the Son of Man did not come to be served, but to serve, and to give his life as a ransom for many."

Even God Himself—the One who deserves everything—didn't come to be served. If I saw God in the flesh, I don't know what I would do, but I don't think letting Him serve me would be my first reaction. I hope that it would be to offer Him everything I have—to give back to Him everything He's given me and then be amazed at what He is able to do with it.

If you think about it, that's what Jesus did. He came to give and serve and do His Father's will. But where did Jesus choose to serve and spend the majority of His time? The Pharisees don't forget to mention it multiple times: it was with tax collectors, the poor, the sinners, the sick, the outcasts, the lepers, the cheaters, the prostitutes, the worst of the worst. He didn't just hang out with these people; He was constantly serving them. He healed them, talked with them, preached to them, and occasionally even fed them. He served. His whole point of coming to this earth wasn't to be served but to give His life as a ransom for many.

What does that word *ransom* mean to you? When I look at the verse, that word stands out to me. *Ransom.* It makes me think about a hostage situation, when the kidnappers ask for ransom money. Like with the pirate attacks off the Somalia coast, for example. It is something that fades in and out of the news. When people give ransom money in situations like that, most of the time those taken hostage are given back—set free.

> Jesus lived to give. He lived His life to give it for us.

How did Jesus ransom us? The Bible tells us that we were dead in our transgressions (Ephesians 2:5). That means we were taken hostage with a debt that we could never pay. No amount of money could ever pay back the ransom we owed because of sin. No amount of good deeds—even living a life of giving—could ever cover it. We needed someone to *do something.* That someone, that person who paid the debt, was Jesus. He gave His life as a ransom for you and me.

Jesus lived to give. He lived His life to give it for us. That's one way we can truly be like Christ! Our lives can have the same focus and the same point: giving.

BE INTENTIONAL

We've talked about living to give, but to be honest with you, I didn't used to think about why I was living. Then watching that World Vision DVD about the little girl in Africa with my family woke me up. I started to ask myself what keeps me going day after day. What are those things? God, my family, the support of my friends, but also people like Ignatious.

Ignatious is a child from Uganda whom I have been sponsoring for over nine years now. Ignatious really made a difference in my life by writing me letters whenever he got the chance. I still get letters from him. Ignatious has also taught me an important lesson. It is the lesson of this book—a lesson I have learned from people like George and so many others. It is the lesson of being intentional about your journey.

What was my intention? To make a difference. I just wanted to do something. I wanted Ignatious to know that on the other side of the world, someone cared about him.

When World Vision goes into a village, they try to leave it better than when they came in. At some point, World Vision leaves the area, which means the children being sponsored no longer need support. It is an amazing day, but when it happened in Ignatious's village, it was an incredibly hard day for me.

Here is what Ignatious had to say about our intentional journey in the last letter I got from him:

Dear Sponsor Austin,

Special greetings in the name of our Lord Jesus Christ. I am so happy and grateful to Him that together with the community we have benefitted a lot from your support through World Vision. I used to move a long distance for medical care but now we are able to access treatment from nearer. God bless you. Very soon, World Vision is going to serve another area . . . we might not communicate again but spiritually remain together.

Your Sponsored Child,

Ignatious

This letter meant so much to me. He sounds almost excited to see and know that another community is going to be reached and blessed. He is excited to see more intentional giving take place. World Vision had a set purpose in going into the community. Even though that community's need may have seemed overwhelming, they did the job. Ignatious said it himself: he now has medical care he used to not have. An intentional act changed the world for him and his neighbors.

This is so much a part of what we've been talking about throughout this book. By sitting down and figuring out who you are, what gifts God has packed in your lunch, and how best to go about using them for Him, you're turning what was once an idea into reality, a little bit at a time. You fix your eyes on a direction and go toward it!

I was on a constant journey with my sponsorship of Ignatious. Each month I gave money to support him. When I was younger, my allowance went to Ignatious. Now, looking back, I can see how a little bit really does go a long way.

Being intentional is also about being prepared. Because I wanted to help my friend Ignatious, I asked for my parents' help and learned how to budget the "little bit" I had. Budgeting is a way of being prepared for rainy days or tough times. When we prepare for setbacks and learn how to bounce back from them, we're making sure our resources, our time, and our lunches get where they need to go. And who knows where that may end up being!

A LITTLE GOES A LONG WAY

I had the chance to meet Ignatious a few years back, and all I can say is *wow*! On top of everything we'd learned from each other over the years, Ignatious taught me even more in the little time I spent with him in Africa. But one of the lessons I remember most from that time is that the size of our journey doesn't matter. Your little bit really does go a long way. Ignatious showed me what had happened through my years of support. He was in school and doing well. He was able to purchase two pigs, start a garden, have a bike, and have health care. He was able to even move to a home closer to the local market. Ignatious was able to have a future. Why? Because our family didn't worry about how far the journey would go—only that we started on that journey—a little bit at a time. Ignatious's life was and is forever changed because we started. Our lives are changed forever as well.

Ignatious, you are always on my mind, buddy. If you are reading this, thanks for inspiring me. I will always pray for you and your family. God be with you.

THE STARTING LINE

My final encouragement to you as you are finishing this book is to start where you are. It doesn't matter if it is a journey of one mile, 19.3 miles, or 2,057 miles. You just have to start. When you take a step, you're on your way to seeing amazing things happen. In this book we have talked about so many of the wonderful things that have happened to me, and I get excited just thinking about what your stories might be. So just be ready for what God will do! Be willing to let Him use you and your lunch.

Remember, you were put on this earth for a reason.

Every day is a chance to walk toward that reason—a chance to give.

What needs do you see around you? When you look around, do you see a chance to give? As the old saying goes, "You are blessed to be a blessing." We have been blessed so we can bless. This begins when we keep an eagle eye out for opportunities to give, and when we train our hearts on God and His love for others. So look at your life!

As I mentioned before, the sight of homeless people on the side of the street always pulls at my heart. The signs they often hold have something written on them like, "Anything helps." If anything does help, the few quarters rolling around in your car can help. They can help make a difference for that one man or woman. Your time can help. Your talents can help. A life of giving begins by looking for those opportunities every day. A lifetime's worth of stories starts with just one step, one handful of coins, one word of encouragement to someone in need, one hoop shot for hope, one small lunch given to a Miracle-Maker. You have that power right now!

Prayer is a key ingredient in finding those opportunities. God will open up doors for us if we allow Him to—if we ask Him to. He wants to use us, so let's be ready at all times. Today, right this minute, pray for God to show you these doors in your life. I'm praying with you and for you. Will you join me?

Dear God,

Thank You for the gifts You've given me and for choosing to use me—for letting me be a part of Your plan for the world. God, I want to live to give, so the very first thing I want to give to You is my trust. Today, please show me what my gifts are and how You want me to use them to make a difference. Where is the need? How can I help? What's the first step? Please stir up passion in my heart. Protect me from setbacks and squashers, bless me with supporters, and fill me with the joy and determination that come from seeing something through even when it's hard. God, I want to see the world changed for You! Thank You for guiding my steps as I walk through the doors You open. In Jesus' name, Amen.

••••••◦━◦••••••

All in all, living begins by giving. If we can give, we will feel a new sense of living. So let's do more than just walk the earth every day. It is time to bless. It is time to give. It is time to be extraordinary—no matter how old or young we may be. So, let's go! A new life, a giving life, awaits. To truly live . . . we give.

Notes

Chapter 1: Live to Give

1. World Food Programme, "Hunger Stats," accessed February 19, 2012, http://www.wfp.org/hunger/stats.
2. Matthew 14:13–21; Mark 6:30–44; Luke 9:10–17; John 6:5–15.
3. Emphasis added.
4. Bible Exposition, "The Feeding of the Five Thousand," accessed May 9, 2012, http://www.dabhand.org/Essays/NT511%20Feeding.htm.

Chapter 3: Different Outside and In

1. Karl S. Kruszelnicki, "Fingerprints of Twins," ABC Science, accessed February 19, 2012, http://www.abc.net.au/science/articles/2004/11/04/1234875.htm.
2. For instance, try www.spiritualgiftstest.com for a good youth test. Your church might even have its own test. Do some digging and check it out!
3. Andy Andrews, *The Butterfly Effect* (Nashville: Thomas Nelson, 2010).

4. "Little Foxes," accessed February 5, 2012, http://www
.moreillustrations.com/Illustrations/small%20things%202
.html.

Chapter 5: Don't Lose Your Lunch!
1. Global Rich List, www.globalrichlist.com.
2. Adrienne Villani, "How Rich Are You," *Beyond Profit* (blog), May 27, 2010, accessed February 19, 2012, http://beyondprofit.com/how-rich-are-you.
3. *Spider-Man*, directed by Sam Raimi (Burbank, CA: Columbia Pictures, 2002), DVD. See also Luke 12:48.
4. *Batman Begins*, directed by Christopher Nolan (Burbank, CA: Warner Brothers, 2005), DVD; *The Dark Knight*, directed by Christopher Nolan (Burbank, CA: Warner Brothers, 2008), DVD.

Chapter 6: Grab Your Lunch and Hit the Road
1. "Dehydration Directory," WebMD, accessed February 19, 2012, http://www.webmd.com/a-to-z-guides/dehydration-directory.

Chapter 8: Your Biggest Fear: Fear
1. This was a SurveyMonkey poll of my Facebook friends. They were from different religious backgrounds but with a strong Christian presence, both guys and girls of all ages.
2. Orphan's Hope, accessed February 19, 2012, http://www.orphanshope.org/our_vision.html.

Chapter 11: Sandwich Squasher
1. "Assessment Procedures of Bullying," accessed April 18, 2012, http://www.teachsafeschools.org/bully_menu3.html.
2. "Test Your Bullying Knowledge," accessed February 19, 2012, http://www.stopbullying.gov/topics/what_is_bullying/test_your_knowledge/.

Acknowledgments

I would like to give thanks to:

God

Grace

My amazing parents, Dan and Denise

My incredible sister, Brittany

My loving grandparents, Gary and Sharon, Don and Judy

My late great-grandmother, Joyce Megason, or as I know her . . . Grammy

My fantastic editors, MacKenzie and Jenn

And our generation

About the Author and Hoops of Hope

At the age of nine, Austin Gutwein was moved when he learned there were more than 15 million children orphaned by HIV/AIDS, with 12 million living in sub-Saharan Africa. Austin decided he had to do his part. He decided to make a difference for just one orphan—one free throw at a time.

In 2004, Austin went to his school gymnasium and

shot 2,057 free throws representing the 2,057 children who would lose their parents during one school day. Now in its eighth year, Austin's basketball marathon organization, Hoops of Hope, has spread around the world. Austin's passion has motivated more than 40,000 kids, teens, and adults to make a difference. Austin and Hoops of Hope have raised more than $3 million for orphaned children in Africa.

As of 2012, Hoops of Hope events have taken place in more than thirty countries and built two medical clinics, a high school, four dormitories, and a computer lab in rural Zambia; two Hope Centers in Swaziland; a water project in Kenya; and a school in India. They have provided hundreds of bicycles and supplied medical clinics with more than a thousand medical caregiver kits to assist HIV/AIDS-infected parents with the basic supplies they need to live longer so they can provide for their children. The money Hoops of Hope has raised has kept thousands of children in Africa from becoming orphans. But the story doesn't stop there. Hoops of Hope continues to grow and inspire people all across the world. Check out what Hoops of Hope has been up to lately at hoopsofhope.org.

In September of 2009, Thomas Nelson Publishers released Austin's first book, *Take Your Best Shot*. In the first year alone, the book exceeded expectations by selling more than 75,000 copies worldwide.

In the past few years, Austin has shared his message of hope that anyone can make a difference to more than 500,000 people who live throughout Europe, the Middle East, Africa, China, Canada, and the United States. He has been a keynote speaker on the Revolve Tour and Women of Faith, at several concerts and tours, churches, and schools, as well as the United States Air Force Academy.

Since founding Hoops of Hope, Austin has been awarded the Prudential Spirit of Community Service Award, the Baron Prize for Young Heroes, the Build-a-Bear Huggable Heroes Award, and the Tempe World of Difference Award. In 2009, he was selected as one of the top ten most caring Americans by the Caring Institute for his work on behalf of AIDS orphans.

Austin and his story have been featured in magazines as well as in the national broadcast and electronic news, including CBS Sports' NCAA pregame coverage, NBC's *Today Show*, the *NBC Nightly News*, *CBS Evening News*, *Time for Kids*, and *Christianity Today*.

Now eighteen, Austin serves as chair on the Arizona Governor's Youth Commission and continues to speak and inspire his generation to make a difference.

In the fall of 2012, Austin is attending Anderson University in Anderson, Indiana, where he plans to pursue a degree in political science. Although many lives have been improved through Austin's efforts with

Hoops of Hope, the impact of his message is still to be determined, as he continues to share and lead his generation to make a difference, to take their best shot, and to live a life of giving.